ON

THE AESTHETIC EDUCATION

OF MAN

ON
THE AESTHETIC EDUCATION
OF MAN

IN A SERIES OF LETTERS

by

FRIEDRICH SCHILLER

TRANSLATED WITH AN INTRODUCTION

BY REGINALD SNELL

FREDERICK UNGAR PUBLISHING CO.

NEW YORK

Republished 1965

First published 1954
by Routledge & Kegan Paul Ltd

Seventh Printing, 1983 ,

Printed in the United States of America

ISBN 0-8044-6819-2

Library of Congress Catalog Card No. 65-28262

Contents

INTRODUCTION	*page* 1
FIRST LETTER	23
SECOND LETTER	25
THIRD LETTER	27
FOURTH LETTER	30
FIFTH LETTER	34
SIXTH LETTER	37
SEVENTH LETTER	45
EIGHTH LETTER	47
NINTH LETTER	50
TENTH LETTER	55
ELEVENTH LETTER	60
TWELFTH LETTER	64
THIRTEENTH LETTER	67
FOURTEENTH LETTER	73
FIFTEENTH LETTER	75
SIXTEENTH LETTER	81
SEVENTEENTH LETTER	85
EIGHTEENTH LETTER	87
NINETEENTH LETTER	91
TWENTIETH LETTER	97
TWENTY-FIRST LETTER	100
TWENTY-SECOND LETTER	102
TWENTY-THIRD LETTER	107
TWENTY-FOURTH LETTER	113
TWENTY-FIFTH LETTER	119
TWENTY-SIXTH LETTER	124
TWENTY-SEVENTH LETTER	131
INDEX	141

Introduction

IT may help the general reader to a fuller understanding of these important and not always easy Letters if they are first set before him in their proper historical and philosophical context. In one sense, to be sure, they need neither explanation nor commentary; they were published without the help of either—but the time and the circumstances of their publication provided both. It does not finally matter in what year they first saw the light; they are, as every genuine work of art must be, always contemporary. They were not written for any particular time, but they were inevitably written at a particular time. (Even if they had been written only for that time, they would still be immensely worth our attention today, so closely do the cultural and political problems of Schiller's age resemble our own; I shall make no attempt to underline the parallels, which every attentive reader will find sufficiently striking.) When we say that something was published in 1795 we have mentioned more than a mere date—the work in question demands to be read in the light of the events that were stirring the Europe of that day. Again, these Letters have their place in the history of philosophy; the student of aesthetics already knows of them, at least by hearsay. They are not, indeed, professional philosophy, and it is not positively necessary to know more than the everyday meanings of some of the technical terms which

Schiller employs; but to say that any man wrote a semi-philosophical work under the strong influence of Kant and Goethe is more than merely mentioning names as sign-posts. The reader who has no interest in either history or philosophy may skip the paragraphs that follow without serious loss to his enjoyment of Schiller's *Aesthetic Letters*, and certainly without missing anything historically or philosophically profound. The sketching-in of their background will be of the slightest, but enough, I hope, to satisfy the barest requirements of the student. Here, then, are the time, the circumstances, and the climate of philosophical opinion in which these Letters first appeared.

THE HISTORICAL BACKGROUND OF THE LETTERS

In 1793 the poet, who was then thirty-three years of age, and had already held the post of Professor of History at Jena University for four years, wrote a series of letters to a Danish Prince, Friedrich Christian of Schleswig-Holstein-Augustenburg, on the subject of aesthetic education. This enlightened man had generously helped Schiller a couple of years previously, when he had been disappointed in his work and was suffering from the first attack of the illness that was finally to prove fatal to him; he invited the poet to his court, promising him a government post when he should have fully regained his health, and, when this proved impracticable, he conferred on him a pension of one thousand thalers annually for three years, with no stipulation attached to the gift except that 'he should be careful of his health and use every attention to recover'. The letters were the first fruits of that recovery. The subject of them was much in Schiller's mind at the time: Kant's celebrated *Critique of Judgement* had been published in 1790, and he was beginning to take the

2

Kantian philosophy seriously; further, he was himself giving a course of lectures on aesthetics at Jena, and had already published several essays including *On the cause of pleasure in tragic objects, On the art of tragedy, On grace and dignity, On the sublime,* as well as the *Kallias* letters on Beauty (in fact, of his chief aesthetic writings, only the most famous, the treatise *On naive and sentimental poetry,* was of a later date than the Letters here translated). Whether or not they were intended for publication, they never reached a wider circle than the Copenhagen court, for all the originals were destroyed by a fire at the Prince's palace in 1794; but copies of some of them survive, which Friedrich Christian had made to forward to interested friends, and of the original series of nine, seven are printed in some complete editions of Schiller's works. Believing in the importance of what he had to say, he later remodelled and rewrote the whole series, nearly doubling their length, and began to publish them by instalments in the newly founded journal *The Graces,* which he was editing. Schiller's aesthetic philosophy was immediately accepted among his colleagues, and became the artistic banner of the distinguished group of writers who contributed to *The Graces* —a group which included such well-known names as Goethe, Herder, Kant, Fichte, the Humboldts, the Schlegels, Klopstock, and Jacobi. These men proved, indeed, too distinguished to be at all tractable as literary collaborators, and the contents of the journal were persistently above the heads of the readers for whom it was intended; it collapsed after three years of brilliant and erratic existence—not the last venture of its kind to start with excellent auspices and unexceptionable aims, to give publication to first-rate work (it printed Goethe's splendid *Roman Elegies*) and then quietly to fizzle out. The original series of letters roughly corresponded to Letters 1–11 and 24–27 here

3

translated (though Nos. 3 and 4 are new in matter—the discourse on the relationship of State and individual), Nos. 11–23 on the two fundamental impulses being worked out at much greater length than the original plan allowed for; much of the contents of the first four Letters is word for word the same as in the original series.

The influence of contemporary historical events upon the argument of the Letters is obvious. Schiller had begun to write them during the Reign of Terror in France; when he uses such terms as Freedom or Ideal Man, they must be read in the light of the events that were shaking not only Paris but all thinking Europeans. Friedrich Christian and his circle had embraced the humanitarian ideals of the Revolution with enthusiasm, and in the original letters Schiller's own radical sympathies are more obvious than in the final version here translated. A good deal had happened in the two intervening years, and the later tone of political disillusion is significant. The poet knew that some declaration of freedom was required of him, but, like an inverted Balaam, he could not pronounce any unqualified blessing upon its most recent manifestation; if he did not exactly curse it, he made it clear that in his view mankind must first learn to serve Beauty before it could faithfully serve Freedom—the world, he felt, was not ready for political liberty, and it was necessary to prepare for a true conception of it by developing first a sense of the beautiful. That is, in fact, the whole theme of the Letters.

SCHILLER'S PLACE IN AESTHETIC PHILOSOPHY

Though these Letters are not a strictly philosophical work, Schiller occupies a recognizable and not unimportant place in the history of aesthetic philosophy. Aesthetics has been called 'the German science', and the phrase does enshrine a half-truth: the bibliography of essays, dissertations, doctor's theses and full-scale philosophical treatments of this subject that have appeared in Germany during the last two hundred years must far exceed that of any other three nations put together. But the Germans are a little too apt to think of other people's aesthetic theories as merely amateur. That is, perhaps, the right title for some of our own countrymen, such as Addison and Burke, who have contributed to the subject, but *vixerunt fortes ante* Baumgarten, and Corneille and Boileau (to say nothing of Plato and Aristotle) had said some not insignificant things about the Beautiful. What is true is that the word aesthetics itself first takes on its modern meaning, to denote a particular branch of philosophy, in the *Aesthetica* of Alexander Gottlieb Baumgarten, first published in 1750, a few years before Schiller was born; and that the subject does seem to hold a peculiar attraction, not only for German *Gelehrte* but for German poets—one thinks immediately of Gottsched, Lessing, the two Schlegels, Novalis, and even of Richard Wagner. (Kant protested at the time at this application of a term which was already current in his own philosophical system in another—and in the light of Greek linguistic usage quite legitimate—sense, to the 'new' branch of philosophy, but Baumgarten's usage finally won popular acceptance in the teeth of learned opposition. If Sir William Hamilton had had his way, we should be calling the subject *apolaustics*.) Schiller himself was a creator rather than a theorizer, but he possessed a first-rate intellect—his nearest English counterpart in this respect is Shelley—and all his philosophical writing, which is considerable both in extent and in importance, is a blend of poetic imagery and ratiocination. When he thinks abstractly, he can sometimes think very clearly indeed; but he is not happy for

5

long in the intense inane. Von Humboldt once said to him: 'Nobody can say whether you are the poet who philosophizes, or the philosopher who makes poetry,' and Schiller himself was well aware that he could not sustain the role of either pure thinker or pure poet for long at a time. 'I want,' he wrote to Fichte, 'not merely to make my thoughts clear to another, but to surrender to him at the same time my whole soul, and to influence his sensuous powers as well as his intellectual.' It is this duality in him that will always cause some lovers of poetry to find his poetry, and some lovers of abstract thought to find his philosophy, in some degree repellent; but there will always be fortunate people who are prejudiced by neither against the other, and rejoice in what is fine in both. He clearly felt the strain of preserving the requisite balance in his nature: 'While the philosopher may allow his imagination, and the poet his power of abstraction to rest, I am obliged when working in this manner [he is referring to precisely the kind of writing illustrated in these Letters] to maintain both of these powers in an equal state of tension, and only by a constant movement within me can I keep the two heterogeneous elements in a kind of solution.' [1] His general estimate of himself as a poet-thinker is both modest and shrewd: in a previous letter to Goethe, early on in their acquaintance, he had written: 'Do not expect to find any great store of ideas in me . . . My mind works in a symbolizing way, and so I hover, like a kind of hybrid, between concept and contemplation, between law and feeling, between a technical mind and genius. It is this that gave me, particularly in earlier years, a somewhat awkward appearance both in the field of speculation and in that of poetry; for the poetic mind generally got the better of me when I ought to have philosophized, and my philosophical

[1] From a letter to Goethe, 16th October 1795.

6

spirit when I wanted to be a poet. Even now it happens frequently enough that imagination interferes with my abstractions, and cold intellect with my poetry.' [1] But he managed to forge a prose style that was admirably adapted to its twofold purpose—Jean Paul called it 'the perfection of pomp-prose'; at times, indeed, the antitheses, the elaborately balanced periods, are almost overdone, but it is always good German prose of its century.

PHILOSOPHICAL INFLUENCES ON SCHILLER

As I have already suggested, Schiller was somewhat loosely attached to contemporary philosophical schools; he was primarily a creative writer—lyric poet, imaginative historian, dramatist. But his interest in philosophy was both genuine and deep. It was Kant's system that had a profounder effect on him than any other, and the increase in profundity in his own aesthetic writings closely follows his increasing understanding of Kant. His least important writings on this subject belong to his pre-Kantian period; he wrote the *Kallias* letters when he was busy with *The Critique of Judgement*; and the essay *On grace and dignity*, the Letters here translated, and *On naive and sentimental poetry*, representing his most fully developed aesthetic views, all date from the time when he had assimilated the Kantian philosophy. (This was precisely the time when he was in almost daily contact with the mind of Goethe, and those two powerful influences, though by no means exerted in the same direction, are sometimes a little difficult to separate.) Yet he never claimed to be a strict disciple of Kant. 'In the cardinal question of moral theory,' he told Prince Friedrich Christian, 'my thought is completely Kantian'; he was as much attracted as Goethe was repelled by Kant's

[1] 31st August 1794.

7

moral approach to art. He admittedly took from Kant the twofold conception of Man as sensuousness and reason; very Kantian, too, is his declaration to Körner that 'The Beautiful is not an inductive idea, but rather an imperative'. It was a casual remark of Kant's that art, compared with labour, may be considered as play, that originally prompted him to develop his own theory of the play impulse set forth in these Letters, but he rejected much of this master's asceticism and moral rigour—Schiller would always have put Love of God above Obedience to Law. In a sense, indeed, Schiller's play impulse is only an elaboration of the view propounded in the *Critique of Judgement*, where play means all that is not internally or externally contingent, nor yet constrained—the expression of a nature whose two fundamental tendencies (in the Kantian sense) are fully harmonized and poised, so that the aesthetic-creative impulse cannot develop until the play impulse is in easy and habitual action. But Schiller is nearer Fichte than Kant in his distinction between Subject and Object, and in his view of their necessarily reciprocal operation; he quotes Fichte twice, in the fourth and thirteenth Letters, and he took over Fichte's 'pure ego' and 'empirical ego' entirely, rechristening them Person and Condition.[1] There are, in addition, numerous echoes of Fichtean thought throughout the Letters.

It might be possible to pursue the whole history of aesthetic thought, and hardly find a single philosopher of standing to whom Schiller was not in some way indebted. He is a true eclectic: classicist by training and intellectual sympathy, romanticist by literary affiliation and native genius, in turn Platonist and Aristotelian. The Platonism is obvious; and the germ of his theory of the simultaneous bracing and relaxing effect of Beauty is surely to be found

[1] Eleventh Letter.

in the sixth book of the *Nicomachean Ethics*, in Aristotle's analogy of the tuning of a lyre. Schiller's own enthusiasm for aesthetics dates from his early youth; and the theme of these Letters, the education of Man through the instrument of Art, had been a favourite topic all his life—it is touched on in his school essays, elaborately discussed in his first writings on the influence of the stage, expounded again and again, with much eloquence, in his poetry, before it was set forth here in the full maturity of his powers. Again, the influence of Montesquieu is obvious; the picture of primitive, aesthetically unawakened, man is pure Rousseau; and it is clear that he has read his Baumgarten, his Mendelssohn, his Burke and his Hume with profit. The influence of Lessing is strong, and that of Winckelmann still stronger—indeed, Schiller's Hellenism is Winckelmann-Hellenism all through, and he looks upon the ancients with the ardent gaze of that eccentric genius. Winckelmann's astonishingly influential book, *The History of Antique Art*, whose publication was so nicely timed by the *Zeitgeist* to have the maximum effect upon a world that wanted just that book—it came neither a decade too early nor a decade too late—had appeared when Schiller was six years old. Its theme was the 'noble simplicity and serene greatness' of classical art, and Schiller did not, and could not, know that the greater part of the sculpture regarded by Winckelmann as Greek was in fact Roman copy, often degenerate at that. His attempt, in one of his early aesthetic writings, to see the Apollo Belvedere and the Laocoon of Rhodes as representatives of a single style will strike us nowadays as quaint; while his reference to the culture that developed 'under Pericles and Alexander' in the tenth of these Letters has an innocent vagueness that makes us wonder how much he really knew about the Greeks. But it may at least be said that his enthusiasm was not so heady as that of many distinguished men of his time, and it is in any case impossible to appreciate Schiller without understanding the importance to him of the classical ideal, the Hellenic manner of life and forms of art, what he took to be the fructifying unity of their activity and their will.[1]

More important than all the influences mentioned, of course, is that of Goethe; the writing of the first Letter dates, almost within a month or two, from the beginning of that remarkable ten-years-long personal and poetical-philosophical association which was the most rewarding, as it is the best known, of all literary partnerships. Schiller was at this time in constant touch with Goethe; he was reading *Wilhelm Meister* in instalments throughout the period of the composition of the Letters (as those who know that work will be occasionally reminded); and Goethe's influence is at least implicit all the way through his argument, becoming explicit in his account of the triumph of art, in his exaltation of the 'natural', in his reverent attitude towards the antique, in his view of the artist as the true man, the unity of the sensuous and the spiritual.

I shall be sorry if I have given the impression that Schiller, in these Letters, is merely the mouthpiece of other men's views. He was an eclectic, but he was much more than a magpie; he has solid virtues as a thinker, although his thought can at no point claim to be original (the thought of very few people can, though much of it insistently does). He always refused to departmentalize Man, and sees him as an organic whole; he sees morality in particular as the exercise of the whole man, and not as some peculiar secretion of a part of him; and his dynamic

[1] It is a pleasure to refer the reader to Prof. E. M. Butler's admirable book *The Tyranny of Greece over Germany*, which is full of good things, well said, upon this subject.

view of education, including—but not confined to—the theory of the possibility of moral education through the refinement of the aesthetic sensibility, will bear comparison with that of the profoundest thinkers on the subject. His poetry and his philosophy are all of a piece; his notion of art as the awakener of human culture, through the liberation of man from desire, and as leading him to ultimate perfection, is first clearly set forth in his poem *The Artists*, and a complete aesthetic philosophy is suggested in the famous *Hymn to Joy* and in *The Gods of Greece*. A passage in the preface to his play *The Bride of Messina* declares that 'the only true art is that which produces the greatest pleasure. The greatest pleasure is the freedom of our nature in the lively exercise of all its powers.' He says somewhere that 'poetry can be to Man what love is to the hero. She can neither advise him, nor strike blows on his behalf, nor do any other office for him. But she can educate him to be a hero. She can summon him to action and furnish him with strength for all that he ought to be.' In case these citations of the names of great predecessors and contemporaries have given the impression that Schiller was only a picker-up and skilful re-hasher of considerable trifles from other men's banquets, I cannot end this section better than by quoting from the Preface to Hegel's *Philosophy of Fine Art*, to shew that one eminent philosopher, at least, had a high regard for Schiller as a thinker. Hegel here pays a warm tribute to 'the artistic sense of a profound, and at the same time philosophic, mind which demanded and proclaimed the principle of totality and reconciliation as against that abstract infinity of thought, that duty for duty's sake, that formless intelligence . . . [meaning the Kantian system] before the time at which it was recognized by technical philosophy'. 'It is Schiller', he goes on, 'to whom we must give credit for the great service of having broken through the Kantian subjectivity and abstractness of thought, daring to transcend them by intellectually apprehending the principles of unity and reconciliation as the truth, and realizing them in art.' It is one of the most remarkable testimonies ever made by a professional philosopher to an amateur.

THE THEME OF THE LETTERS

The whole burden of the argument in these Letters is, in a single sentence, that Man must pass through the aesthetic condition, from the merely physical, in order to reach the rational or moral. The aesthetic condition itself has no significance—all it does is to *restore* Man to himself, so that he can make of himself what he wills. He is a cipher; but he is capable of becoming anything (Schiller here treats art much as Kant did religion). Sensuous Man, then, must become aesthetic Man before he can be moral Man. Schiller develops his theme in a somewhat roundabout way—or rather, in several ways at once—in a series of oppositions and syntheses which sometimes appear to be (and indeed are) mutually inconsistent. The original series of letters represented mankind as capable of existing on different levels, those of Nature, Taste and Reason; the rational State and the moral Man are the ideal, and freedom simply means moral freedom. In the end the natural State was to 'wither away', and Beauty was thus to be the handmaid of pure intellectual culture. The whole argument of those letters was based on the antithesis between Nature (representing multiplicity, content, the realm of phenomena—the demand of Feeling) and Reason (representing unity, form, the realm of morality—the demand of Consciousness). Sometimes Schiller saw these three levels historically: first comes harmonious Nature (typified by the Greeks), then the antagonism of forces and disintegration of human personality (ourselves), and finally renewed wholeness (the perfect Man yet to come). In his theory of the two fundamental impulses, Schiller connects Man's sensuous nature with the material impulse, and his reason with the formal impulse. The former, which rules him as physical being, lays upon him the shackles of physical necessity, and seeks to make him (in Fichtean phrase) pure Object; the latter comes to his rescue from the Absolute, and is capable of leading him back to the Absolute. So Man is a creature of two worlds, urged in two opposite directions at once—to the empirical, the contingent, the subjective on the one hand, and to the free, the necessary (the necessity of the autonomous moral law), the objectively valid on the other. He has to satisfy the demands of both capacities and somehow bring them into harmony with one another; and this he does through the aesthetic, which unites matter and form, sensuousness and reason. Not until he has achieved that harmony is he free; he is a slave so long as he obeys only one of the impulses. How he sets about this in actual practice, Schiller finds it difficult to say. Elsewhere in his writings he emphasizes the importance of the relaxation of Man's powers, especially when they have been one-sidedly employed, and claims that such relaxation is given in its purest form by aesthetic contemplation, which occupies the whole of his powers in the same way that play does; he stresses the opportunity afforded by art, and especially by tragedy, for the exercise of moral power; and he believes that art is capable of introducing that condition of *contentment* (if the word is not misleading; *equipoise* might express it better) which is conducive to his physical and spiritual well-being alike.

I have said that these Letters are not a piece of professional philosophy, and it may be unfair to criticize them as such. Schiller has the faults, no less than the advantages (which are very real) of the amateur philosopher; he is wholly unwilling to use a consistent terminology, and the reader must not expect it of him, here or anywhere else in his philosophical writings. To take only a couple of examples: he will refer to the Godhead indiscriminately as God, Spirit, the Eternal, the Absolute, the Infinite, the Highest Idea, Substance, and even Nature. And this last word, within the compass of these Letters alone, will be found to mean at least eight different things—individuality; creation; *mere* Nature (= blind force); Nature personified (= Mother Nature); harmony (the opposite of our fissiparous culture); wholeness ('his behaviour must *be* Nature'—see the fourth letter); Nature as Idea, the pure concept 'condition of Nature', an abstraction in the mind of Man; multiplicity (as opposed to Reason or unity)— as well as, of course, various mixtures of all these several meanings. No, it is not fair to criticize this work for what it is not; it is as much a piece of feeling as of thinking—a passionate attempt, by gazing at the opposites of reason and sensuousness, freedom and caprice, mind and Nature, duty and inclination, absolute and finite, activity and passivity, the formal impulse and the material impulse (Kantian duality permeates his whole thought now), to grasp the unity lying behind them. But it is fair—indeed, if the reader is not to finish these Letters in a state of bewilderment, it is quite necessary—to point out that even as a piece of feeling it contains a central ambiguity. Schiller often complained, in letters to friends, that the public did not understand what he was aiming at in his argument. He was surely himself to blame, for not making his leading ideas sharper and clearer, in particular the distinction between artistic and moral culture. We are entitled to ask if his 'aesthetic play' is the same as moral beauty, the ideal of humanity, or merely a means of reaching it; we are entitled to complain that he sometimes regards aesthetic culture as the highest conceivable level of human attainment, sometimes merely as the level immediately preceding that of moral culture; and we shall scarcely fail to observe that he never in fact completes the historical enquiry which he begins early in the Letters, concerning the relation between aesthetic and political culture. I do not think it is possible to defend Schiller against this charge of an absolutely central inconsistency. No attentive reader can fail to observe two distinct strata in his argument; what is odder, the two are not separate, but intermingled; and oddest of all, Schiller himself seems quite unaware of it. He is presenting, at the same time, a Three Levels theory of aesthetic development, and a Synthesis theory—and he is mixing them up. (Roughly speaking, we meet the former in the second, third, fifth, eighth, ninth, tenth and sixteenth Letters, the latter in the fourth, sixth, seventh, ninth, eleventh to fifteenth, and seventeenth to twenty-seventh.) In one, Beauty is merely a means of enlightenment, of transitory value; in the other, an end in itself, a work of the reason, of absolute value. In the one, Nature is 'mere' Nature, something to be overcome; in the other, an absolute value. In the one, the conception of freedom is moral, rigorist, Kantian; in the other, freedom is 'aesthetic play'. In the one, the ideal of humanity is purely intellectual, rational Man; in the other, sensuous-rational Man harmonized with himself. In the one, cultural history is an educative process, proceeding

15

from Nature through Taste to Reason; in the other it is a necessary development, the antagonism of the forces of Nature and Reason producing the final synthesis of Beauty. I conceive only one explanation to be possible: that Schiller was simply not aware how profoundly his whole method of thinking was changing, during the months when he was occupied in writing these Letters, so that he allowed whole pages of the original series to stand in a new context which would not actually support them. The writing of this final series of Letters was concomitant with Schiller's own extremely rapid transition to dialectical thinking, which was not, perhaps, fully achieved even with the publication of the last of them; and the risk he took, in launching upon a work like this during such a private intellectual revolution, was aggravated by the necessity for publication by instalments in *The Graces*.

THE SIGNIFICANCE OF THE LETTERS

Why, then, after such criticism and such admissions as the above, do I nevertheless commend these Letters to the attention of every educated person? The answer is simple: as a piece of philosophical thinking they may be gravely faulty, as an essay in sustained argument they may be occasionally perplexing, but as an educational manifesto they are pure gold. The faults to which I have drawn attention above do not finally matter; they should not affect our estimate of the value of their central thesis— they certainly do not detract in the slightest degree from the admiration which I have come to feel increasingly with increasing familiarity with the text, in the course of translating and commenting on these Letters. That thesis is as old as Plato and as new as Herbert Read; and it enshrines more fundamental truth about education than any other which the mind and the heart of man have yet conceived. To quote Herbert Read: 'It is surely one of the curiosities of the history of philosophy that one of the most cherished notions of this great man [Plato] has never been taken seriously by any of his followers, Schiller alone being an exception. Scholars have played with his thesis as with a toy: they have acknowledged its beauty, its logic, its completeness; but never for a moment have they considered its feasibility. They have treated Plato's most passionate ideal as an idle paradox, only to be understood in the context of a lost civilization. The thesis is that art should be the basis of education.'[1] This is not the place to set forth the theory of education through art in detail—it has been done three times, by Plato (especially in *The Republic*, III, 401 ff., and VII, 536, *The Laws*, II, 653-6, and VII, 797-816, and the *Protagoras*, 326), by Schiller in the volume that the reader now holds in his hand, and by Herbert Read in the book from which I have already quoted.[2] But its influence upon the main stream of European education has been negligible—indeed, almost non-existent. We meet traces of it, to be sure, at the Renaissance, in the theory of the architect Leone Battista Alberti of Venice, and the practice of that great schoolmaster Vittorino da Feltre of Mantua; we find it discussed and recommended in Pestalozzi's *Wie Gertrud ihre Kinder lehrt* and in Herbart's *Allgemeine Pädagogik*; and it certainly

[1] Herbert Read: *Education through Art* (Faber, 1943), p. 1. If the publication of these Letters of Schiller in English does nothing further than send a few readers to Herbert Read's great book, it will have been worth doing; for my part, I regard it as 'surely one of the curiosities' of contemporary cultural history that so few educators have been impressed by the wisdom contained in the educational writings of this distinguished poet, critic, and thinker.

[2] And again, very briefly, in a pamphlet entitled *The Education of Free Men* (Freedom Press, 1944), where the statement of it occupies a bare twenty-nine pages.

informed both the theory and practice of Froebel and Jacques Dalcroze (the latter being an *anima naturaliter Platonica*, since he lighted upon this doctrine of art as the handmaid of education quite spontaneously). But it is true to say that the main tendency of humanist education has consistently and persistently ignored it, that our schools—those 'abattoirs of sensibility', in Herbert Read's withering phrase—have, with rare exceptions, simply not begun to explore the possibilities of aesthetic education. I cannot pretend that these letters of Schiller will form a practical handbook to any such attempt, but they should certainly help to inspire it; I hope that their noble eloquence, and the passionate and extremely clear-headed conviction that shines through their occasionally baffling technical formulation (for in spite of Schiller's disavowals it is there, and it takes some disentangling), will lead some readers at least to pursue their topic further, and go back to Plato and forward to Herbert Read. All three of them are concerned to say one simple thing: that (to quote *Education Through Art* once more) 'the aim of imaginative education . . . is to give the individual a concrete sensuous awareness of the harmony and rhythm which enters into the constitution of all living bodies and plants, which is the formal basis of all works of art, to the end that the child, in its life and activities, shall partake of the same organic grace and beauty. By means of such education we instil into the child that "instinct of relationship" which, even before the advent of reason, enables it to distinguish the beautiful from the ugly, the good from the evil, the right pattern of behaviour from the wrong pattern, the noble person from the ignoble.' [1]

After completing my translation of these Letters, I made

[1] Op cit., p. 70.

18

it my business to discover if other English translations existed. There are two: one by J. Weiss (1845), the other in Bohn's Standard Library (1875), reprinted in the Harvard Classics series (1912). I have carefully compared them with each other and with the German text, and the fact that they are both unobtainable makes it easier to say that they are both unreliable; the second of them is incomplete, and they both contain serious distortions—even direct negations—of Schiller's meaning, sometimes of his actual words. The worst jargon is employed by the Bohn volume (which is indeed on occasion quite unintelligible), and the later American reissue faithfully reproduces its remarkable howlers. This criticism of other people's wares in no way implies a high opinion of the merits of my own, which I present simply as a rendering, as nearly literal as may be, of this important work of Schiller's intellectual maturity—I am probably more conscious of its shortcomings than anyone else, but the important thing is that the work should be available at the present time, when its doctrine will possibly be more acceptable than formerly.

I have to acknowledge the valuable help of my colleague, the late Dr. Curt Bromberg, in the elucidation of a number of difficulties in the argument of the Letters. That the translation is no better is no fault of his; I owe it to his watchfulness that it is no worse—I have profited greatly from his humane scholarship and wide philological knowledge.

The text which I have followed is that of the earliest edition of the Letters in book form, in a volume of *Lesser prose writings by Schiller, compiled and corrected by the author himself, from several journals* (Leipzig, 1801). It differs only slightly from the version published in the previous decade in *The Graces*; most of the alterations were to give greater clarity of statement, some small typographical errors were rectified, and Schiller dropped a number of somewhat pedantic footnotes, whose loss the present reader need not regret. From the *Graces* version I have retained only the motto from Rousseau which the poet originally chose to introduce his argument. All the unsigned footnotes here printed are Schiller's. I have added a very few of my own, where comment or explanation seemed to be called for.

R. S.

On the Aesthetic Education
of Man

'Si c'est la raison qui fait l'homme,
c'est le sentiment qui le conduit'

ROUSSEAU

First Letter

so you are willing to allow me to lay before you, in a series of letters, the results of my enquiries into Beauty and Art. I am keenly sensible of the importance, but also of the charm and dignity, of such an undertaking. I shall be speaking of a subject which is closely related to the better portion of our happiness, and not far removed from the moral nobility of human nature. I shall be pleading the cause of Beauty before a heart that perceives and exercises her whole power, and, in an enquiry where one is compelled to appeal as often to feelings as to principles, will take upon itself the heaviest part of my labour.

What I would have begged as a favour you generously lay upon me as a duty, and impute to me the appearance of a service where I am simply yielding to my inclination. The freedom of procedure which you prescribe is no constraint, but rather a necessity for me. Being little practised in the employment of formal terminology, I shall scarcely run the risk of offending against good taste by any misuse of it. My ideas, drawn rather from the uniform familiarity with my own self than from a rich experience of the world, or acquired through reading, will not deny their origin; they will sooner incur any reproach than that of sectarianism, and sooner collapse from their own feebleness than maintain themselves by means of authority and borrowed strength.

I will, to be sure, not conceal from you the fact that it is Kantian principles upon which the propositions that follow will for the most part be based; but you must attribute it to my incapacity, not to those principles, if in the course of these enquiries you should be reminded of any particular school of philosophy. No, I shall regard the freedom of your mind as inviolable. Your own sensibility will furnish the facts upon which I build; your own free intellectual power will dictate the laws by which we shall proceed.

Concerning those ideas which predominate in the practical part of the Kantian system it is only the philosophers who are at variance; I am confident of shewing that mankind as a whole has from the remotest times been in agreement about them. You have only to free them from their technical formulation, and they will emerge as the time-honoured utterances of common reason, and as data of that moral instinct which Nature in her wisdom appointed as Man's guardian until clear insight should bring him to maturity. But it is just this technical formulation, which reveals the truth to our understanding, that conceals it once again from our feeling; for unfortunately the understanding must first destroy the objects of the inner sense before it can appropriate them. Like the chemist, the philosopher finds combination only through dissolution, and the work of spontaneous Nature only through the torture of Art. In order to seize the fleeting appearance he must bind it in the fetters of rule, dissect its fair body into abstract notions, and preserve its living spirit in a sorry skeleton of words. Is it any wonder if natural feeling does not recognize itself in such a likeness, and if truth appears in the analyst's report as paradox?

I too must therefore crave some measure of forbearance if the following enquiries should remove their object from the sphere of sense in attempting to approximate it to the understanding. What is true of moral experience must be true, in a still higher degree, of the manifestation of Beauty. Its whole enchantment lies in its mystery, and its very essence is extinguished with the extinction of the necessary combination of its elements.

Second Letter

BUT should I not, perhaps, be able to make better use of the liberty which you are granting me, than to engage your attention upon the arena of Fine Art? Is it not at least unseasonable to be looking around for a code of laws for the aesthetic world, when the affairs of the moral world provide an interest that is so much keener, and the spirit of philosophical enquiry is, through the circumstances of the time, so vigorously challenged to concern itself with the most perfect of all works of art, the building up of true political freedom?

I should not care to be living in another century, or to have worked for another. We are citizens of an age, as well as of a State; and if it is held to be unseemly, or even inadmissible, for a man to cut himself off from the customs and manners of the circle in which he lives, why should it be less of a duty, in the choice of his activity, to submit his decision to the needs and the taste of his century?

But this decision seems to turn out by no means to the advantage of Art, at least the Art at which alone my enquiries are going to be directed. The course of events has given a direction to the spirit of the age which threatens to remove it even further from the Art of the Ideal. This Art must abandon actuality and soar with becoming boldness above necessity; for Art is a daughter of Freedom, and must receive her commission from the needs of spirits, not from the exigency of matter. But today Necessity is master, and bends a degraded humanity beneath its tyrannous yoke. *Utility* is the great idol of the age, to which all powers must do service and all talents swear allegiance. In these clumsy scales the spiritual service of Art has no weight; deprived of all encouragement, she flees from the noisy mart of our century. The very spirit of philosophical enquiry seizes one province after another from the imagination, and the frontiers of Art are contracted as the boundaries of science are enlarged.

The eyes of the philosopher are fixed as expectantly as those of the worldling upon the political arena where at present, so it is believed, the high destiny of mankind is being decided. Would it not betray a culpable indifference to the welfare of society not to share in this universal discourse? And nearly as this great action, because of its tenor and its consequences, touches everyone who calls himself a man, so, because of its method of procedure, it must especially interest every independent thinker. A question which was formerly answered only by the blind right of the stronger is now, it appears, being brought before the tribunal of pure reason, and anyone who is capable of putting himself in a central position, and raising his individuality to the level of the race, may regard himself as an assessor at this court of reason, seeing that he is an interested party both as human being and as citizen of the world, and finds himself implicated, to a greater or lesser degree, in the issue. Thus it is not simply his own cause that is being decided in this great action; judgement is to

26

be given according to laws which he, as a rational spirit, is himself competent and entitled to dictate.

How attractive it would be for me to conduct an enquiry into such a subject with one who is as genial a thinker as he is a liberal citizen of the world, and to press home the decision to a heart that is dedicated with a fine enthusiasm to the welfare of humanity! What an agreeable surprise, in spite of the difference of worldly station and the wide separation made necessary by the circumstances of the actual world, to meet your unprejudiced mind as it arrives, on the field of ideas, at the same conclusions as my own! The fact that I am resisting this delightful temptation, and allowing Beauty to have precedence of Freedom, I believe I can not merely defend by inclination but justify on principle. I hope to convince you that this subject is far less alien to the need of the age than to its taste, that we must indeed, if we are to solve that political problem in practice, follow the path of aesthetics, since it is through Beauty that we arrive at Freedom. But this proof cannot be adduced until I have reminded you of the principles by which Reason is in general guided in political legislation.

Third Letter

NATURE begins with Man no better than with the rest of her works: she acts for him where he cannot yet act as a free intelligence for himself. But it is just this that constitutes his humanity, that he does not rest satisfied with what Nature has made of him, but possesses the capacity of retracing again, with his reason, the steps which she anticipated with him, of remodelling the work of need into a work of his free choice, and of elevating physical into moral necessity.

He comes to himself out of his sensuous slumber, recognizes himself as Man, looks around and finds himself—in the State. An unavoidable exigency had thrown him there before he could freely choose his station; need ordained it through mere natural laws before he could do so by the laws of reason. But with this State based on need, which had arisen only from his natural endowment as Man, and was calculated for that alone, he could not and cannot as a moral being rest content—and woe to him if he could! With the same right, therefore, by which he becomes a man, he leaves the dominion of a blind necessity, since he is parted from it at so many other points by his freedom, as—to take only a single example—he effaces through morality and ennobles through Beauty the low character which the needs of sexual love imprinted on him. He thus artificially retraces his childhood in his maturity, forms for himself a *state of Nature* in idea, which is not indeed given him by experience but is the necessary result of his rationality, borrows in this ideal state an ultimate aim which he never knew in his actual state of Nature, and a choice of which he was not then capable, and proceeds now exactly as though he were starting afresh and substituting the status of independence, with clear insight and free resolve, for the status of contract. However artfully and firmly blind Lawlessness has laid the foundations of her work, however arrogantly she may maintain it and with whatever appearance of veneration she may surround it—he may regard it during this operation as something that has simply never happened; for the work of blind forces possesses no authority before which Freedom need bow, and everything must yield to the highest ultimate aim which Reason sets up in his personality. In this way the attempt of a people that has reached maturity to transform its natural State into a moral one, originates and vindicates itself.

This natural State (as we may call every political body whose organization is ultimately based on force and not on laws) is now indeed opposed to the moral man, for whom mere conformity to law is now to serve as law; but it is still quite adequate for the physical man, who gives himself laws only in order to come to terms with force. But the physical man is *actual*, and the moral man only *problematical*. Therefore when Reason abolishes the natural State, as she inevitably must do if she wishes to put her own in its place, she weighs the physical and actual man against the problematical moral man, she ventures the very existence of society for a merely possible (even if morally necessary) ideal of society. She takes from Man something that he actually possesses, and without which he possesses nothing, and assigns to him in its place something which he could and should possess; and if she has relied too much upon him she will, for a humanity which is still beyond him and can so remain without detriment to his existence, have also wrested from him those very means of animality which are the condition of his humanity. Before he has had time to hold fast to the law with his will, she has taken the ladder of Nature from under his feet.

The great consideration is, therefore, that physical society in *time* may not cease for an instant while moral society is being formed in *idea*, that for the sake of human dignity its very existence may not be endangered. When the mechanic has the works of a clock to repair, he lets the wheels run down; but the living clockwork of the State must be repaired while it is in motion, and here it is

29

a case of changing the wheels as they revolve. We must therefore search for some support for the continuation of society, to make it independent of the actual State which we want to abolish.

This support is not to be found in the natural character of Man, which, selfish and violent as it is, aims far more at the destruction than at the preservation of society; as little is it to be found in his moral character, which *ex hypothesi* has yet to be formed, and upon which, because it is free and because it is never apparent, the lawgiver can never operate and never with certainty depend. The important thing, therefore, is to dissociate caprice from the physical and freedom from the moral character; to make the first conformable with law, the second dependent on impressions; to remove the former somewhat further from matter in order to bring the latter somewhat nearer to it —so as to create a third character which, related to these other two, might pave the way for a transition from the realm of mere force to the rule of law, and, without impeding the development of the moral character, might serve rather as a sensible pledge of a morality as yet unseen.

Fourth Letter

THIS much is certain: only the predominance of such a character among a people can complete without harm the transformation of a State according to moral principles, and only such a character too can guarantee its perpetuation. In the establishment of a moral State the ethical law is reckoned upon as an active power, and free will is drawn into the realm of causes where everything coheres with strict necessity and stability. But we know that the dispositions of the human will always remain fortuitous, and that only with absolute Being does physical coincide with moral necessity. If therefore we are to count upon the moral conduct of Man as upon *natural* consequences, it must *be* his nature, and Man must be led by his very impulses to such a mode of life as only a moral character can have for its result. But the will of Man stands completely free between duty and inclination, and no physical compulsion can or may encroach upon this sovereign right of his personality. If therefore he is to retain this capacity for choice and nevertheless be a reliable link in the causal concatenation of forces, this can only be achieved if the operations of both those motives in the realm of phenomena prove to be exactly similar, and if the subject matter of his volition remains the same through every variation of its form, so that his impulses are sufficiently consonant with his reason to have the value of a universal legislation.

Every individual man, it may be said, carries in disposition and determination a pure ideal man within himself, with whose unalterable unity it is the great task of his existence, throughout all his vicissitudes, to harmonize.[1] This pure human being, who may be recognized more or less distinctly in every person, is represented by the *State*, the objective and, so to say, canonical form in which the diversity of persons endeavours to unite itself. But two different ways can be thought of, in which Man in time

---

[1] I may refer at this point to a recently published writing by my friend Fichte: *Lectures on the Vocation of the Scholar*, where the reader will find some very luminous inferences from this proposition, that have never before been attempted along these lines.

can be made to coincide with Man in idea, and consequently as many in which the State can affirm itself in individuals: either by the pure man suppressing the empirical—the State abrogating the individual—or by the individual *becoming* State—temporal Man being raised to the dignity of ideal Man.

It is true that on a partial moral estimate this distinction disappears, for Reason is satisfied when her law alone prevails unconditionally; but on a complete anthropological estimate, in which content counts as well as form, and living feeling at the same time has a voice, the distinction is all the more evident. Reason indeed demands unity, but Nature demands multiplicity, and both systems of legislation lay claim to Man's obedience. The law of the former is impressed upon him by an incorruptible consciousness, the law of the latter by an ineradicable feeling. It will therefore always argue a still defective education if the moral character can assert itself only through the sacrifice of what is natural; and a political constitution will still be very imperfect if it is able to produce unity only by suppressing variety. The State should respect not merely the objective and generic, but also the subjective and specific character of its individuals, and in extending the invisible realm of morals it must not depopulate the realm of phenomena.

When the mechanical artist sets his hand to the formless block, to give it the form that he intends for it, he does not hesitate to do it violence, for Nature, which he is fashioning, merits no consideration for herself, and his concern is not with the whole for the sake of the parts, but with the parts for the sake of the whole. When the fine artist sets his hand to this same block, as little does he hesitate to do it violence, only he forbears to shew it. He respects the material at which he works not in the slightest degree more than the mechanical artist does; but he will try to deceive the eye which takes the freedom of this material under its protection, by an apparent deference towards the material. The situation is quite different with the pedagogic and political artist, who has Man at the same time as his material and as his theme. Here his aim reverts to the material, and only because the whole subserves the parts may the parts submit to the whole. The statesman-artist must approach his material with a quite different respect from that which the fine artist feigns towards his; not merely subjectively, and for a delusive effect upon the senses, but objectively, for its inner being, he must pay careful heed to its idiosyncrasy and its personality.

But just for that very reason, because the State is to be an organization which is formed by itself and for itself, it can really become such only insofar as the parts have been severally attuned to the idea of the whole. Because the State serves as a representation of pure and objective humanity in the breast of its citizens, it will have to maintain towards those citizens the same relationship in which they stand to each other, and it can respect their subjective humanity only in such degree as this is exalted to objectivity. If the inner man is at one with himself, he will preserve his idiosyncrasy even in the widest universality of his conduct, and the State will be simply the interpreter of his fine instinct, the clearer expression of his inner legislation. On the other hand, if in the character of a people the subjective man is opposed to the objective in so contradictory a fashion that only the suppression of the former can secure the triumph of the latter, the State too will assume the full severity of the law against the citizen, and must ruthlessly trample underfoot any such hostile individuality in order not to be its victim.

33

But Man can be at odds with himself in a double fashion: either as savage if his feelings rule his principles, or as barbarian if his principles destroy his feelings. The savage despises Art and recognizes Nature as his sovereign mistress; the barbarian derides and dishonours Nature, but—more contemptible than the savage—he continues frequently enough to become the slave of his slave. The cultured man makes a friend of Nature and respects her freedom while merely curbing her caprice.

When therefore Reason introduces her moral unity into physical society, she must not injure the multiplicity of Nature. When Nature strives to maintain her multiplicity in the moral structure of society, there must be no rupture in its moral unity; the triumphant form rests equidistant from uniformity and confusion. *Totality* of character must therefore be found in a people that is capable and worthy of exchanging the State of need for the State of freedom.

Fifth Letter

IS this the character which the present age and contemporary events reveal to us? I direct my attention at once to the most prominent object in this vast picture.

It is true that deference to authority has declined, that its lawlessness is unmasked, and, although still armed with power, sneaks no dignity any more; men have awoken from their long lethargy and self-deception, and by an impressive majority they are demanding the restitution of their inalienable rights. Nor are they merely demanding them: on every side they are bestirring themselves to seize by force what has, in their opinion, been wrongfully withheld from them. The fabric of the natural State is tottering, its rotten foundations are yielding, and there seems to be a *physical* possibility of setting Law upon the throne, of honouring Man at last as an end in himself and making true freedom the basis of political association. Vain hope! The *moral* possibility is wanting, and the favourable moment finds an apathetic generation.

Man portrays himself in his deeds, and what a form it is that is depicted in the drama of the present day! Here barbarity, there enervation: the two extremes of human degeneracy, and both of them united in a single period of time!

Among the lower and more numerous classes we find crude, lawless impulses which have been unleashed by the loosening of the bonds of civil order, and are hastening with ungovernable fury to their brutal satisfaction. It may be that objective humanity had some cause of complaint concerning the State; subjective humanity must respect its institutions. Can we blame the State for disregarding the dignity of human nature so long as it was defending its very existence, for hastening to separate by the force of gravity, and to link together by the force of cohesion, where there could as yet be no thought of building up? The extinction of the State contains its vindication. Society uncontrolled, instead of hastening upwards into organic life, is relapsing into its original elements.

On the other hand, the civilized classes present to us the still more repugnant spectacle of indolence, and a depravity of character which is all the more shocking since culture itself is the source of it. I forget which ancient or modern philosopher made the remark that what is more noble is in its corruption the more abominable; [1] but it is equally true in the moral sphere. The child of Nature, when he breaks loose, becomes a maniac, the disciple of Art an abandoned wretch. The intellectual enlightenment on which the refined ranks of society, not without justification, pride themselves, reveals on the whole an influence upon the disposition so little ennobling that it rather furnishes maxims to confirm depravity. We disown Nature in her rightful sphere only to experience her tyranny in the sphere of morality, and in resisting her influences we receive from her our principles. The affected propriety of our manners refuses her the first vote—which would have been pardonable—only to concede to her, in our materialistic moral philosophy, the decisive final say. Selfishness has established its system in the very bosom of our exquisitely refined society, and we experience all the contagions and all the calamities of community without the accompaniment of a communal spirit. We submit our free judgement to its despotic sanction, our feeling to its fantastic customs, our will to its seductions; only our caprice do we assert against its sacred rights. Proud selfsufficiency contracts, in the worldling, the heart that often still beats sympathetically in the rude natural man, and like fugitives from a burning city everyone seeks only to rescue his own miserable property from the devastation. Only in a complete abjuration of sensibility may we think to find protection against its abuse, and the ridicule which is often the salutary chastener of the fanatic, lacerates the noblest feelings with equally little consideration. So far from setting us free, culture only develops a new want with

[1] The saying is sometimes attributed to St. Thomas Aquinas, who in *Sum. Theol.*, 2ᵃ, 2ᵃᵉ, Qu. 34, Art. 2, translates a passage in Aristotle (*Nic. Eth.* VIII, 10, 2) as *optimo oppositum pessimum*. But the most usual form of the saying, *corruptio optimi pessima*, is probably proverbial. —*Trans.*

every power that it bestows on us; the bonds of the physical are tightened ever more alarmingly, so that the fear of loss stifles even the burning impulses towards improvement, and the maxim of passive obedience passes for the supreme wisdom of life. So we see the spirit of the time fluctuating between perverseness and brutality, between unnaturalness and mere Nature, between superstition and moral unbelief, and it is only the equilibrium of evil that still occasionally sets bounds to it.

Sixth Letter

HAVE I perhaps overdone this description of the age? I do not anticipate that objection, but rather a different one: that I have proved too much by it. This picture, you will tell me, certainly resembles contemporary humanity, but it also resembles any people at all that is in process of civilization, since all without distinction must fall away from Nature through over-subtlety of intellect before they can return to her through Reason.

But if we pay any attention to the character of the age we must be astonished at the contrast we shall find between the present form of humanity and the bygone one, in particular the Greek. Our reputation for culture and refinement, which we justly stress in considering every mere state of Nature, will not serve our turn in regard to the Greek nature, which united all the attractions of art and all the dignity of wisdom, without, however, becoming the victim of them as does our own. The Greeks put us to shame not only by their simplicity, which is alien to our age: they are at the same time our rivals, often indeed our models, in those very excellences with which we are wont to console ourselves for the unnaturalness of our manners. Combining fullness of form with fullness of content, at once philosophic and creative, at the same time tender and energetic, we see them uniting the youthfulness of fantasy with the manliness of reason in a splendid humanity.

At that time, in that lovely awakening of the intellectual powers, the senses and the mind had still no strictly separate individualities, for no dissension had yet constrained them to make hostile partition with each other and determine their boundaries. Poetry had not yet courted wit, and speculation had not prostituted itself by sophistry. Both of them could, if need arose, exchange their functions, because each in its own fashion honoured truth. However high Reason might soar, it always drew its subject matter lovingly after it, and however fine and sharp the divisions it made, it never mutilated. It certainly split up human nature, and scattered its magnified elements abroad among the glorious assembly of the gods, but not by tearing it in pieces, rather by combining it in varying ways; for the whole of humanity was never lacking in any single god. How completely different it is with us moderns! With us too the image of the race is scattered on an amplified scale among individuals—but in a fragmentary way, not in different combinations, so that you have to go the rounds from individual to individual in order to gather the totality of the race. With us, one might almost be tempted to assert, the mental faculties shew themselves detached in operation as psychology separates them in idea, and we see not merely individual persons but whole classes of human beings developing only a part of their capacities, while the rest of them, like a stunted plant, shew only a feeble vestige of their nature.

I do not fail to appreciate the advantages to which the present generation, considered as a unity and weighed in the scales of reason, may lay claim in the face of the best of antiquity, but it has to enter the contest in close order and let whole compete with whole. What individual modern will emerge to contend in single combat with the individual Athenian for the prize of humanity?

Whence comes this disadvantageous relation of individuals in spite of all the advantages of the race? Why was the individual Greek qualified to be the representative of his time, and why may the individual modern not dare to be so? Because it was all-uniting Nature that bestowed upon the former, and all-dividing intellect that bestowed upon the latter, their respective forms.

It was culture itself that inflicted this wound upon modern humanity. As soon as enlarged experience and more precise speculation made necessary a sharper division of the sciences on the one hand, and on the other, the more intricate machinery of States made necessary a more rigorous dissociation of ranks and occupations, the essential bond of human nature was torn apart, and a ruinous conflict set its harmonious powers at variance. The intuitive and the speculative understanding took up hostile attitudes upon their respective fields, whose boundaries they now began to guard with jealousy and distrust, and by confining our activity to a single sphere we have handed ourselves over to a master who is not infrequently inclined to end up by suppressing the rest of our capacities. While in one place a luxuriant imagination ravages the hard-earned fruits of the intellect, in another the spirit of abstraction stifles the fire at which the heart might have warmed itself and the fancy been enkindled.

This disorder, which Art and learning began in the inner man, was rendered complete and universal by the new spirit of government. It was not, indeed, to be expected that the simple organization of the first republics would outlive the ingenuousness of their early manners and conditions; but instead of rising to a higher animal life it degenerated to a common and clumsy mechanism. That zoophyte character of the Greek States, where every individual enjoyed an independent life and, when need arose, could become a whole in himself, now gave place to an ingenious piece of machinery, in which out of the botching together of a vast number of lifeless parts a collective mechanical life results. State and Church, law and customs, were now torn asunder; enjoyment was separated from labour, means from ends, effort from reward. Eternally chained to only one single little fragment of the whole, Man himself grew to be only a fragment; with the monotonous noise of the wheel he drives everlastingly in his ears, he never develops the harmony of his being, and instead of imprinting humanity upon his nature he becomes merely the imprint of his occupation, of his science. But even the meagre fragmentary association which still links the individual members to the whole, does not depend on forms which present themselves spontaneously (for how could such an artificial and clandestine piece of mechanism be entrusted to their freedom ?), but is assigned to them with scrupulous exactness by a formula in which their free intelligence is restricted. The lifeless letter takes the place of the living understanding, and a practised memory is a surer guide than genius and feeling.

If the community makes function the measure of a man, when it respects in one of its citizens only memory, in another a tabulating intellect, in a third only mechanical skill; if, indifferent to character, it here lays stress upon knowledge alone, and there pardons the profoundest darkness of the intellect so long as it co-exists with a spirit of order and a law-abiding demeanour—if at the same time it requires these special aptitudes to be exercised with an intensity proportionate to the loss of extension which it permits in the individuals concerned—can we then wonder that the remaining aptitudes of the mind become neglected in order to bestow every attention upon the only one which brings in honour and profit? We know indeed that vigorous genius does not make the boundaries of its concern the boundaries of its activity; but mediocre talent consumes the whole meagre sum of its strength in the concern that falls to its lot, and it must be no ordinary head that has something left over for private pursuits without prejudice to its vocation. Moreover, it is seldom a good recommendation with the State when powers exceed commissions, or when the higher spiritual requirements of the man of genius furnish a rival to his office. So jealous is the State for the exclusive possession of its servants, that it will more easily bring itself (and who can blame it?) to share its man with a Cytherean than with a Uranian Venus! [1]

And so gradually individual concrete life is extinguished, in order that the abstract life of the whole may prolong its sorry existence, and the State remains eternally alien to its citizens because nowhere does feeling discover it. Compelled to disburden itself of the diversity of its citizens by means of classification, and to receive humanity only at second hand, by representation, the governing section finally loses sight of it completely, confounding it with a mere patchwork of the intellect; and the governed cannot help receiving coldly the laws which are addressed so little towards themselves. Finally, weary of maintaining a bond which is so little alleviated for it by the State, positive society disintegrates (as has long since been the fate of the majority of European States) into a moral state of

[1] As presiding over earthly and spiritual love respectively.—*Trans.*

Nature, where open force is only one *more* party, hated and eluded by those who make it necessary, and respected only by those who can dispense with it.

With this twofold force pressing on it from within and without, could humanity really take any other course than the one it actually has taken? While the speculative spirit strove after imperishable possessions in the realm of ideas, it had to become a stranger in the material world, and relinquish matter for the sake of form. The business spirit, confined in a monotonous circle of objects, and inside these still further restricted by formulas, was forced to see the freedom of the whole snatched from under its eyes, and at the same time to become impoverished in its own sphere. As the former is tempted to fashion the actual according to the conceivable, and to exalt the subjective conditions of its imagination into laws constituting the existence of things, so the latter plunged to the opposite extreme of estimating all experience whatsoever by a particular fragment of experience, and trying to apply the rules of its own occupation indiscriminately to every occupation. One fell a victim to a vain subtlety, the other to a narrow pedantry, because the former stood too high to see the individual, and the latter too low to see the whole. But the deleterious effect of this tendency of mind was not restricted to knowledge and utterance alone; it extended not less to feeling and action. We know that the sensibility of the mind depends for its degree upon the liveliness, and for its extent upon the richness, of the imagination. But the predominance of the analytical faculty must necessarily deprive the fancy of its strength and its fire, and a restricted sphere of objects must diminish its wealth. Hence the abstract thinker very often has a *cold* heart, since he analyses the impressions which really affect the soul only as a whole; the man of business has very often a *narrow* heart, because his imagination, confined within the monotonous circle of his profession, cannot expand to unfamiliar modes of representation.

I have been concerned to reveal the pernicious tendency of our contemporary character and its source, not to shew the advantages by which Nature makes amends for it. I will gladly concede to you that, little as individuals could derive any profit from this dismemberment of their being, yet the race could have made progress in no other way. The phenomenon of Greek humanity was undoubtedly a maximum which could neither be maintained at that pitch nor be surpassed. Not maintained, because the intellect was inevitably bound to be compelled by the store which it already possessed to dissociate itself from sensation and contemplation, and to strive after clearness of knowledge; and also not surpassed, because only to a certain degree is clarity compatible with fullness and warmth. This degree the Greeks had attained, and if they wanted to advance to a higher state of development they were, like ourselves, obliged to surrender the wholeness of their being and pursue truth along separate roads.

There was no other way of developing the manifold capacities of Man than by placing them in opposition to each other. This antagonism of powers is the great instrument of culture, but it is only the instrument; for as long as it persists, we are only on the way towards culture. Only by individual powers in Man becoming isolated and arrogating to themselves an exclusive right of legislation, do they come into conflict with the truth of things and compel popular opinion, which ordinarily rests with indolent satisfaction upon outward appearance, to penetrate the depth of objects. While the pure intellect usurps authority in the world of sense, and the empirical intellect is engaged in subjecting it to the conditions of experience, both capacities develop to the utmost degree of maturity and exhaust the whole extent of their sphere. While in one the imagination dares, through its caprice, to dissolve the universal order, in the other it compels the reason to climb to the highest sources of knowledge, and to summon to aid the law of necessity against that order.

Partiality in the exercise of powers, it is true, inevitably leads the individual into error, but the race to truth. Only by concentrating the whole energy of our spirit in one single focus, and drawing together our whole being into one single power, do we attach wings, so to say, to this individual power and lead it artificially beyond the bounds which Nature seems to have imposed upon it. As surely as all human individuals, taken together, with the power of vision which Nature has granted them, would never succeed in observing a satellite of Jupiter which the telescope reveals to the astronomer, so beyond question is it that human reflection would never have achieved an analysis of the infinite or a critique of pure reason, unless Reason had become dismembered among the several relevant subjects, as it were wrenched itself loose from all matter and strengthened its gaze into the Absolute by the most intense abstraction. But will such a spirit, resolved, so to say, into pure intellect and pure contemplation, be capable of exchanging the rigid fetters of logic for the free gait of imagination, and of apprehending the individuality of things with just and pure intention? Nature here sets, even to the universal genius, a limit which it cannot pass, and truth will make martyrs so long as philosophy still holds it to be her principal business to provide against error.

Thus, however much may be gained for the world as a whole by this fragmentary cultivation of human powers, it is undeniable that the individuals whom it affects suffer under the curse of this universal aim. Athletic bodies are certainly developed by means of gymnastic exercises, but only through the free and equable play of the limbs is beauty formed. In the same way the exertion of individual talents certainly produces extraordinary men, but only their even tempering makes full and happy men. And in what relation should we stand to past and future ages if the cultivation of human nature made such a sacrifice necessary? We should have been the bondslaves of humanity, we should have drudged for it for centuries on end, and branded upon our mutilated nature the shameful traces of this servitude—in order that a later generation might devote itself in blissful indolence to the care of its moral health, and develop the free growth of its humanity!

But can Man really be destined to neglect himself for any end whatever? Should Nature be able, by her designs, to rob us of a completeness which Reason prescribes to us by hers? It must be false that the cultivation of individual powers necessitates the sacrifice of their totality; or however much the law of Nature did have that tendency, we must be at liberty to restore by means of a higher Art this wholeness in our nature which Art has destroyed.

Seventh Letter

OUGHT we perhaps to look for this action from the State? That is not possible; for the State, as it is now constituted, has brought about the evil, and the State as Reason conceives it in idea, instead of being able to establish this better humanity, must first be itself established by it. And so the foregoing enquiries have brought me back again to the point from which they drew me for a time. The present age, so far from exhibiting to us that form of humanity which we have recognized to be the necessary condition of the moral reform of the State, shews us rather the precise opposite. If, therefore, the principles I have laid down are correct, and experience confirms my description of the present time, we must continue to regard every attempt at reform as inopportune, and every hope based upon it as chimerical, until the division of the inner Man has been done away with, and his nature has developed with sufficient completeness to be itself the artificer, and to guarantee reality to the political creation of Reason.

Nature in her physical creation indicates to us the way we should pursue in moral creation. Not until the struggle of elementary powers in the lower organizations has been assuaged, does she rise to the noble formation of the physical Man. In the same way the strife of elements in the ethical Man, the conflict of blind impulses, must first be allayed, and the crude antagonism within him must have ceased, before we may dare to promote his diversity. On the other hand, the independence of his character must be assured, and subjection to alien despotic forms have given place to a decent freedom, before we can submit the multiplicity in him to the unity of the ideal. Where primitive Man still misuses his caprice so lawlessly, we can hardly disclose to him his freedom; where civilized Man makes so little use of his freedom, we cannot deprive him of his caprice. The gift of liberal principles becomes a piece of treachery to the whole, when it is associated with a still effervescing power and reinforces an already overweening nature; the law of conformity becomes tyranny towards the individual when it is combined with an already prevailing weakness and physical limitation, and so extinguishes the last glimmering sparks of spontaneity and individuality.

The character of the time must first, therefore, recover from its deep degradation; in one place it must cast off the blind force of Nature, and in another return to her simplicity, truth and fullness—a task for more than a single century. Meanwhile, I readily admit, many attempts may succeed in detail, but no improvement in the whole will thereby be achieved, and contradiction of behaviour will always demonstrate against unity of maxims. In other quarters of the globe humanity may be respected in the negro, while in Europe it is dishonoured in the thinker. The old principles will remain, but they will wear the dress of the century, and philosophy will lend its name to an oppression which was formerly authorized by the Church. Terrified of the freedom which always declares its hostility to their first attempts, men will in one place throw themselves into the arms of a comfortable servitude, and in another, driven to despair by a pedantic tutelage, they will break out into the wild libertinism of the natural State. Usurpation will plead the weakness of human nature, insurrection its dignity, until at length the great sovereign of all human affairs, blind Force, steps in to decide the sham conflict of principles like a common prize-fight.

Eighth Letter

is philosophy then to retire, dejected and despairing, from this field? While the dominion of forms is being extended in every other direction, is this most important of all goods to be at the mercy of formless chance? Is the conflict of blind forces to continue for ever in the political world, and is the social law never to triumph over malignant self-interest?

By no means! Reason, it is true, will not attempt an immediate struggle with this brutal power which resists her weapons, and no more than the son of Saturn in the Iliad will she descend to personal combat in the dismal arena. But out of the midst of the combatants she selects the worthiest, arrays him, as Zeus did his grandson, in divine armour and decides the great issue through his victorious strength.

Reason has accomplished all she can, in discovering and expounding Law; it is the task of courageous will and lively feeling to execute it. If Truth is to gain the victory in the struggle with Force, she must first become herself a *force*, and find some *impulse* to champion her in the realm of phenomena; for impulses are the only motive forces in the sensible world. That she has up till now displayed her conquering strength so little, is the fault not of the intellect which was incapable of unveiling it, but of the heart which remained closed to it, and the impulse which refused its aid.

Whence in fact arises this still universal sway of prejudice, and this darkness of thought in the face of all the light that philosophy and experience have shed? The age is enlightened, that is to say knowledge has been discovered and disseminated which would suffice at least to set right our practical principles. The spirit of free enquiry has scattered the erroneous conceptions which for a long time hindered the approach to truth, and is undermining the foundations upon which fanaticism and fraud have raised their throne. Reason has been purged from the illusions of the senses and from a deceitful sophistry, and philosophy itself, which first caused us to forsake Nature, is calling us loudly and urgently back to her bosom—why is it that we still remain barbarians?

There must be something present in the dispositions of men—since it does not lie in things—which obstructs the reception of truth, however brightly it may shine, and its acceptance, however actively it may convince. An ancient sage has felt this truth, and it lies concealed in the significant maxim: *sapere aude.*[1]

Dare to be wise! Energy of spirit is needed to overcome the obstacles which indolence of nature as well a cowardice of heart oppose to our instruction. It is not without significance that the old myth makes the goddess of Wisdom emerge fully armed from the head of Jupiter; for her very first function is warlike. Even in her birth she has to maintain a hard struggle with the senses, which do not want to be dragged from their sweet repose. The greater part of humanity is too much harassed and fatigued by the struggle with want, to rally itself for a new and sterner struggle with error. Content if they themselves escape the hard labour of thought, men gladly resign to others the guardianship of their ideas, and if it happens that higher needs are stirred in them, they embrace with eager faith the formulas which State and priesthood hold in readiness for such an occasion. If these unhappy people earn our sympathy, we should be rightly contemptuous of those others whom a better lot has freed from the yoke of necessity, but their own choice continues to stoop beneath it. These men prefer the twilight of obscure conceptions, where feeling is livelier and fancy fashions comfortable images at its own pleasure, to the beams of truth which dispel the fond delusion of their dreams. On the

[1] Horace, Ep. I, 2, l. 40.—*Trans.*

49

very deceptions which the hostile light of knowledge should dissipate, they have based the whole structure of their happiness, and are they to purchase so dearly a truth which begins by depriving them of everything they value? They would need to be already wise, in order to love wisdom: a truth which was already felt by the man who gave philosophy its name.[1]

It is, therefore, not enough to say that all intellectual enlightenment deserves our respect only insofar as it reacts upon the character; to a certain extent it proceeds from the character, since the way to the head must lie through the heart. Training of the sensibility is then the more pressing need of our age, not merely because it will be a means of making the improved understanding effective for living, but for the very reason that it awakens this improvement.

Ninth Letter

BUT are we perhaps not arguing in a circle? Is theoretical culture to bring about practical culture, and yet the practical is to be the condition of the theoretical? All improvement in the political sphere is to proceed from the ennobling of the character—but how, under the influence of a barbarous constitution, can the character become ennobled? We should need, for this end, to seek out some instrument which the State does not afford us, and with it open up well-springs which will keep pure and clear throughout every political corruption.

[1] Pythagoras.—*Trans.*

I have now reached the point to which all the foregoing considerations have been directed. This instrument is the Fine Arts, and these well-springs are opened up in their immortal examples.

Art, like Science, is free from everything that is positive or established by human conventions, and both of them rejoice in an absolute immunity from human lawlessness. The political legislator can enclose their territory, but he cannot govern within it. He can proscribe the friend of truth, but Truth endures; he can humiliate the artist, but Art he cannot debase. Nothing, it is true, is more common than for both Science and Art to pay homage to the spirit of the age, and for creative taste to accept the law of critical taste. Where character is rigid and obdurate, we see Science keeping a strict watch over its frontiers, and Art moving in the heavy shackles of rules; where character is enervated and loose, Science will strive to please and Art to gratify. For whole centuries now philosophers and artists have shewn themselves occupied in plunging Truth and Beauty in the depths of vulgar humanity; they themselves are submerged there, but Truth and Beauty struggle with their own indestructible vitality triumphantly to the surface.

No doubt the artist is the child of his time; but woe to him if he is also its disciple, or even its favourite. Let some beneficent deity snatch the infant betimes from his mother's breast, let it nourish him with the milk of a better age and suffer him to grow up to full maturity beneath the distant skies of Greece. Then when he has become a man, let him return to his century as an alien figure; but not in order to gladden it by his appearance, rather, terrible like Agamemnon's son, to cleanse it. He will indeed take his subject matter from the present age, but his form he will borrow from a nobler time—nay, from beyond all time, from the absolute unchangeable unity of his being. Here, from the pure aether of his daemonic nature, flows forth the well-spring of Beauty, untainted by the corruption of the generations and ages which wallow in the dark eddies below it. A freak of temper can degrade his matter, as it has dignified it; but the chaste form is removed from its vicissitudes. The Roman of the first century had long bowed the knee before his emperors, while the gods' statues still stood erect; the temples remained holy in men's eyes when the gods had long since become objects of ridicule, and the infamous crimes of a Nero and a Commodus were put to shame by the noble style of the building which lent concealment to them. Humanity has lost its dignity, but Art has rescued and preserved it in significant stone; Truth lives on in the midst of deception, and from the copy the original will once again be restored. As noble Art has survived noble nature, so too she marches ahead of it, fashioning and awakening by her inspiration. Before Truth sends her triumphant light into the depths of the heart, imagination catches its rays, and the peaks of humanity will be glowing when humid night still lingers in the valleys.

But how does the artist secure himself against the corruptions of his time, which everywhere encircle him? By disdaining its opinion. Let him look upwards to his own dignity and to Law, not downwards to fortune and to everyday needs. Free alike from the futile activity which would gladly set its mark upon the fleeting moment and from the impatient spirit of extravagance which applies the measure of the Absolute to the sorry productions of Time, let him resign the sphere of the actual to the intellect, whose home it is; but let him strive, through the union of the possible with the necessary, to produce the Ideal. Let him stamp it on illusion and truth, coin it in the play of his imagination and in the gravity of his actions, in every sensuous and spiritual form, and quietly launch it into infinite Time.

But not everyone with this ideal glowing in his soul has been endowed with creative tranquillity and the great patient temper to imprint it upon the silent stone or to pour it into the sober word and entrust it to the faithful hands of Time. Much too impetuous to proceed by such quiet means as this, the divine creative impulse often plunges immediately into the present and into the practical business of life, and attempts to transform the formless substance of the moral world. The unhappiness of his generation speaks urgently to the sensitive man, its degradation still more urgently; enthusiasm is kindled, and glowing desire strives impatiently for action in vigorous souls. But has he also asked himself whether these disorders in the moral world offend his reason, or whether they do not rather grieve his self-love? If he does not yet know the answer, he will discover it in the eagerness with which he presses for definite and rapid results. The pure moral impulse is directed at the Absolute; time does not exist for it, and the future is its present, as soon as it necessarily develops out of the present. For a reason having no limits direction is also completion, and the road has been travelled when once it has been chosen.

Give then, I shall reply to the young friend of Truth and Beauty who wants to learn from me how he can satisfy the noble impulse in his breast in the face of all the opposition in his century—give the world on which you are acting the *direction* towards the good, and the quiet rhythm of time will bring about its development. You have given it this direction, if by your teaching you elevate its thoughts to the necessary and the eternal, if by your actions or your creations you transform the necessary and eternal into the object of its impulses. The fabric of error and lawlessness will fall, it must fall; it has already fallen as soon as you are certain that it is leaning over; but it must lean in the inner, not merely in the outward man. In the modest stillness of your heart you must cherish victorious truth, display it from within yourself in Beauty, so that not merely thought may pay homage to it, but sense too may lay loving hold on its appearance. And lest by any chance you may receive the pattern you are to give it from actuality, do not dare to enter its doubtful society until you are assured of an ideal following in your heart. Live with your century, but do not be its creature; render to your contemporaries what they need, not what they praise. Without sharing their guilt, share with noble resignation their penalties, and bow with freedom beneath the yoke which they can as ill dispense with as they can bear it. By the steadfast courage with which you disdain their good fortune, you will prove to them that it is not your cowardice that submits to their sufferings. Think of them as they ought to be when you have to influence them, but think of them as they are when you are tempted to act on their behalf. Seek their approbation through their dignity, but impute their good fortune to their unworthiness; thus on the one hand, your own nobility will awaken theirs, and on the other, their unworthiness will not defeat your purpose. The gravity of your principles will scare them from you, but in play they will continue to tolerate them; their taste is purer than their heart, and it is here that you must lay hold of the timorous fugitive. In vain you will assail their maxims, in vain condemn their deeds; but you can try your fashioning hand upon their idleness. Drive away lawlessness, frivolity and coarseness from their pleasure, and you will imperceptibly banish them from their actions, and finally from their dispositions. Wherever you find

54

them, surround them with noble, great and ingenious forms, enclose them all round with the symbols of excellence, until actuality is overpowered by appearance and Nature by Art.[1]

Tenth Letter

so you are at one with me about this, and are convinced by the contents of my previous letters that Man can be drawn aside from his destination in two opposite ways, that our age is actually travelling along both these false roads, and has fallen a prey to coarseness on the one hand, and to enervation and perversity on the other. From this twofold confusion it must be restored by means of Beauty. But how can the cultivation of Beauty encounter these two opposing defects at once, and unite within itself two contradictory qualities? Can it fetter Nature in the savage and set her free in the barbarian? Can it at the same time harness and unleash—and if it does not really manage both, how is it reasonable to expect from it so great a result as the education of humanity?

We are indeed almost tired of having to listen to the assertion that the developed feeling for Beauty refines manners, so that no proof appears to be necessary here. We

[1] In presenting this remarkable portrait of the ideal artist, Schiller evidently had a definite model in his mind, and the discerning reader will probably have guessed who it was. 'You will find in these letters,' he wrote to Goethe on 20th October 1794, 'a portrait of yourself, beneath which I would gladly have written your name, if I did not hate the idea of forestalling the feelings of thoughtful readers. No one whose judgement you can value will mistake it, for I know that I have conceived it well and drawn it faithfully enough.'—*Trans.*

rely upon the daily experience which almost universally shews a cultivated taste to be linked with clearness of intellect, liveliness of feeling, liberality and even dignity of conduct, while an uncultivated one is usually linked with their opposites. We appeal, confidently enough, to the example of the most cultured of all the nations of antiquity, among whom the feeling for Beauty at the same time reached its highest development, and to the opposite example of those partly savage, partly barbarous peoples who pay for their insensibility to Beauty by a coarse or at all events an austere character. Nevertheless, it does occur at times to thinking people either to deny the fact, or at any rate to doubt the legitimacy of the conclusions that may be drawn from it. They do not think quite so badly of that savagery with which the uncultivated peoples are reproached, or quite so favourably of that refinement which is extolled in the cultivated. Even in antiquity there were men who considered liberal culture to be anything but a boon, and were therefore much inclined to deny the imaginative arts an entrance into their republic.

I am not speaking of those who revile the Graces merely because they have never experienced their favour. People who know no other standard of value than the trouble of acquisition and the palpable profit—how should these be capable of appreciating the quiet work of taste in the outward and the inner man, and of not losing sight of its essential advantages among the incidental disadvantages of liberal culture? The man lacking in form despises all grace of diction as corruption, all elegance in social intercourse as hypocrisy, all delicacy and loftiness of demeanour as exaggeration and affectation. He cannot forgive the favourite of the Graces for brightening every circle by his company, for turning all heads towards his designs in public affairs, for impressing his spirit perhaps on his whole century by his writing, while he himself, the victim of drudgery, can with all his knowledge enforce no attention, move no single stone from its place. As he is never capable of learning from his rival the genial secret of being agreeable, there is no choice left him but to bewail the perversity of human nature which pays homage rather to appearance than to reality.

But there are respectable opinions which deny the influence of Beauty, and have armed themselves with formidable arguments against it from experience. 'It is not to be denied', they say, 'that the charms of the Beautiful can in good hands minister to laudable ends; but it does not contradict their essential nature to do exactly the opposite in bad hands, and to employ their soul-captivating power in the interest of error and injustice. Precisely because taste pays heed only to form and never to content, it finally gives the soul a dangerous tendency to neglect all reality entirely and to sacrifice truth and morality to an attractive façade. All distinction of things is lost, and it is merely appearance that determines their worth.' 'How many men of talent', they continue, 'are drawn away from a serious and strenuous activity by the seductive power of Beauty, or at least induced to pursue it very superficially! How many weak intellects are for that reason alone at odds with the organization of society, because it has pleased the fancy of the poets to present a world in which everything follows in quite a different fashion, where convention does not fetter opinion, nor Art hold Nature in subjection. What dangerous dialectic have the passions not studied, since they have been flaunting themselves in the most brilliant colours in the paintings of the poets, and have, in the contest with laws and duties, usually been masters of the field? What has society really gained from the fact that Beauty now gives laws to the social intercourse which was previously controlled by Truth, and that outward impression determines the respect which should attach to merit alone? It is true that we now see all those virtues flourishing which have an agreeable appearance and confer value in society, but on the other hand every kind of excess is rampant, and every vice is current which is compatible with a beautiful exterior.' It must indeed set us thinking when we find that in almost every epoch in history when the arts are flourishing and taste prevails, humanity is in a state of decline, and cannot produce a single example where a high degree and wide diffusion of aesthetic culture among a people has gone hand in hand with political freedom and civic virtue, fine manners with good morals, or refinement with truth of conduct.

So long as Athens and Sparta maintained their independence, and respect for the law was the basis of their constitutions, taste was immature, Art still in its infancy, and Beauty was still far from ruling the hearts of men. The art of poetry, it is true, had already soared to sublime heights, but only on the pinions of genius, which we know to border very closely upon savagery, and to be a light that is apt to shine in the midst of general darkness, so that it is a witness rather against the taste of its time than for it. When under Pericles and Alexander the golden age of Art arrived, and the rule of taste was more generally extended, we cease to find strength and freedom in Greece; eloquence was debasing truth, wisdom gave offence in the mouth of a Socrates and virtue in the life of a Phocion. The Romans, we know, had first to exhaust their strength in the civil wars and, enervated by oriental luxury, to bow beneath the yoke of a successful dynast, before we see Greek art triumphing over the rigidity of their character. Among the Arabs too the light of culture never dawned until the vigour of their warlike spirit had relaxed beneath the sceptre of the 'Abbāsids. In modern Italy, Fine Art did not shew itself until after the grand confederation of the Lombards was broken, Florence had submitted to the Medicis, and the sense of independence in all those high-spirited cities had given place to an inglorious resignation. It is almost superfluous to recall further the examples of the modern nations whose refinement has increased in direct proportion as their independence has declined. Wherever we turn our gaze in the ancient world, we find taste and freedom mutually avoiding each other, and Beauty establishing her sway only on the ruins of heroic virtues.

And yet this very energy of character, at whose price aesthetic culture is usually purchased, is the most powerful mainspring of all that is great and excellent in Man, the lack of which no other advantage, however great, is able to repair. If then we keep solely to what experience has taught us hitherto about the influence of Beauty, we cannot certainly be much encouraged in the development of feelings which are so dangerous to the true culture of mankind; and we should rather dispense with the melting power of Beauty, even at the risk of coarseness and austerity, than see ourselves, with all the advantages of refinement, consigned to her enervating influence. But perhaps experience is not the tribunal before which such a question is to be decided, and before we allow any weight to its testimony it must first be established, beyond doubt, that it is the selfsame Beauty about which we are speaking and against which those examples testify. But this seems to presuppose a conception of Beauty which has some other source than experience, since by this conception we are to discover whether what experience calls beautiful is entitled to the name.

This pure *rational concept* of Beauty, if such a thing may

59

be adduced, can be drawn from no actual case—rather does it itself correct and guide our judgement concerning every actual case; it must therefore be sought along the path of abstraction, and it can be inferred simply from the possibility of a nature that is both sensuous and rational; in a word, Beauty must be exhibited as a necessary condition of humanity. We must therefore rise now to the pure conception of humanity, and as experience shews us only isolated situations of individual human beings, but never humanity, we must discover what is absolute and enduring in these individual and variable manifestations of theirs, and by rejecting all fortuitous barriers endeavour to seize hold of the indispensable conditions of their existence. Certainly this transcendental road will for a time withdraw us from the familiar circle of phenomena and from the living presence of things, to tarry on the bare plain of abstract conceptions; but we are striving, after all, for a firm basis of knowledge, which nothing is ever to shake, and those who do not venture out beyond actuality will never capture Truth.

Eleventh Letter

WHEN abstraction mounts as high as it possibly can, it arrives at two final concepts, at which it must halt and recognize its limits. It distinguishes in Man something that endures and something that perpetually alters. The enduring it calls his *person*, the changing his *condition*.

Person and condition—the self and its determinations—which we think of in the absolute Being as one and the same, are eternally two in the finite. Throughout the persistence of the person the condition changes, through every change of condition the person persists. We pass from rest to activity, from passion to indifference, from assent to contradiction; but *we* always exist, and what springs immediately from ourselves remains. In the absolute Person alone all the determinations persist alongside the personality, since they flow *out* of the personality. All that Divinity is, it is just *because* it is; consequently it is everything to eternity, because it is eternal.

Since in Man, as finite being, person and condition are distinct, neither can the condition be derived from the person nor the person from the condition. In the latter case, the person would have to alter; in the former, the condition would have to persist, and thus in each case either the personality or the finiteness would cease. Not because we think and will and feel do we exist; not because we exist and think and will do we feel. We exist because we exist; we feel, think and will because there is something other besides ourselves.

The person must therefore be its own ground, for the enduring cannot issue from alteration; and so we have in the first place the idea of absolute being grounded in itself, that is to say of *freedom*. Condition must have a ground; since it does not exist through the person, and is thus not absolute, it must *result*; and so we have in the second place the qualification of all dependent being or becoming, *time*. 'Time is the condition of all becoming' is an identical proposition, for it merely asserts that the result is the condition of something resulting.

The person that is revealed in the eternally persisting ego, and only there, cannot become, cannot have a beginning in time; the reverse is rather the case—time must begin in it, because something constant must form the basis of change. There must be something that alters, if alteration is to occur; this something cannot therefore itself be alteration. In saying that the flower blooms and fades, we make the flower the thing that persists through the transformation and lend it, so to say, a personality in which both those conditions are manifested. It is no objection that Man has first to become; for Man is not simply person in general but person situated in a particular condition. But every condition, every definite instance arises in time, and so Man as phenomenon must have his beginning, although the pure intelligence in him is eternal. Without time, that is to say without becoming it, he would never be a definite existence; his personality would certainly exist in potentiality, but not in fact. Only through the succession of its perceptions does the persisting ego itself come to appear.

The subject matter of activity, therefore, or the reality which the supreme Intelligence creates out of itself, must first be *received* by Man, and he does in fact receive it as something external to himself in space and as something changing within himself in time, through the medium of perception. This changing substance in him is accompanied by his never-changing ego—and to remain perpetually himself throughout all change, to turn every perception into experience, that is, into unity of knowledge, and to make each of his manifestations in time a law for all time, is the rule which is prescribed for him by his rational nature. Only as he alters does he *exist*; only as he remains unalterable does *he* exist. Man conceived in his perfection would accordingly be the constant unity which amidst the tides of change remains eternally the same.

Now although an infinite being, a divinity, cannot *become*, we must surely call divine a tendency which has for its infinite task the proper characteristic of divinity, absolute realization of capacity (actuality of all that is possible) and absolute unity of manifestation (necessity of all that is actual). Beyond question Man carries the potentiality for divinity within himself; the path to divinity, if we may call a path what never reaches its goal, is open to him in his *senses*.

His personality, regarded in itself alone and independently of all sense material, is merely the potentiality of a possible infinite expression; and so long as he neither contemplates nor feels he is still nothing but form and empty capacity. His sense faculty, regarded in itself alone and dissociated from all spontaneous activity of the mind, can do nothing beyond making him material—for without it he is mere form—but by no means uniting him to matter. So long as he only perceives, only desires and acts from mere appetite, he is still nothing but *world*, if we understand by this term simply the formless content of time. It is indeed his sense faculty alone which turns his capacity into operative power; but it is only his personality which makes his operation really his own. Thus in order not to be merely world, he must lend form to his material; in order not to be merely form, he must make actual the potentiality which he bears within himself. He realizes form when he creates time, and opposes constancy with alteration, the eternal unity of his ego with the diversity of the world; he gives form to matter when he proceeds to annul time, affirms persistence within change, and subjects the diversity of the world to the unity of his ego.

Hence flow two contrary demands upon Man, the two fundamental laws of his sensuous-rational nature. The first insists upon absolute *reality*: he is to turn everything that is mere form into world, and realize all his potentialities; the second insists upon absolute *formality*: he is to eradicate in himself everything that is merely world, and produce harmony in all its mutations; in other words, he is to turn outward everything internal, and give form to everything external. Both tasks, considered in their supreme fulfilment, lead back to the conception of divinity from which I started.

Twelfth Letter

TO the fulfilment of this twofold task, of bringing what is necessary *within us* to reality, and subjecting what is real *outside us* to the law of necessity, we are urged by two contrary forces which, because they impel us to realize their object, are very properly called impulses. The first of these impulses, which I shall name the *sensuous*, proceeds from the physical existence of Man or from his sensuous nature, and is concerned with setting him within the bounds of time and turning him into matter; not with giving him matter, since that is the province of a free activity of the person, which matter receives and distinguishes from the persisting self. By matter I here mean nothing but alteration, or reality which occupies time; consequently this impulse demands that there should be alteration, that time should have content. This condition of merely occupied time is called sensation, and it is this alone through which physical existence proclaims itself.

As everything in time is *successive*, so the fact that a thing exists excludes everything else. When we touch a note upon an instrument, only this single note among all those which it is capable of emitting is realized; when Man perceives what is present, the whole infinite possibility of his disposition is confined to this single form of existence. So wherever this impulse acts exclusively, there is necessarily present the highest degree of limitation; Man in this condition is nothing but a unit of magnitude, an occupied moment of time—or rather, *he* is not, for his personality is extinguished so long as sense perception governs him and time whirls him along with itself.[1]

The sphere of this impulse is coextensive with the finiteness of Man; and as every form appears only in some material, everything absolute only through the medium of limitations, it is of course the sense impulse in which the whole phenomenon of mankind is ultimately rooted. But although this alone arouses and develops the potentialities of mankind, it is this alone that makes their perfection impossible. It fetters the upward striving spirit with indestructible bonds to the world of sense, and summons abstraction from its freest excursions into the infinite, back into the boundaries of the present. Thought may indeed elude it for the moment, and a firm will may triumphantly oppose its demands; but Nature once rebuffed soon returns to claim her rights, to press for reality of existence, for some content in our perceptions and for purpose in our actions.

The second of these impulses, which we may call the *formal* impulse, proceeds from Man's absolute existence or

[1] Everyday language has for this condition of absence-of-self under the domination of sense-perception the very appropriate expression *to be beside oneself*—that is, to be outside one's ego. Although this phrase only occurs where the perception becomes a passion, and the condition grows more noticeable by reason of its longer duration, yet everyone is beside himself as long as he only perceives. To return from this condition to self-possession is called, equally correctly, *coming to oneself*—that is, returning to one's ego, re-establishing the personality. We do not say of a man who lies in a swoon, *he is beside himself*, but *he has passed out*—that is, he has been deprived of his ego, since he is no longer inside it. Hence a man who recovers from a swoon is only *his own self again*, which is quite compatible with the condition of being beside himself.

from his rational nature, and strives to set him at liberty, to bring harmony into the diversity of his manifestation, and to maintain his person throughout every change of circumstance. As this person, being an absolute indivisible unity, can never be at variance with itself, since we are ourselves to all eternity, that impulse which insists on affirming the personality can never demand anything other than what it must demand to all eternity; it therefore decides for ever as it decides for the moment, and enjoins for the moment what it enjoins for ever. Consequently it embraces the whole time series, which is as much as to say it annuls time and change; it wishes the actual to be necessary and eternal, and the eternal and necessary to be actual; in other words, it aims at truth and right.

If the first impulse only furnishes *cases*, the other gives *laws*: laws for every judgement where knowledge is concerned, laws for every volition where it is a question of action. Whether we recognize an object, and lend objective validity to a subjective condition in ourselves, or whether we act from knowledge, and make something objective the determining principle of our condition, in both cases we snatch this condition away from the juris-diction of time and endow it with reality for all men and all times—that is, with universality and necessity. Feeling can only say: this is true *for this person* and *at this moment*, and another moment, another person may come to withdraw the assertion of the present sensation. But when once thought pronounces: *that is*, it decides for ever and aye, and the validity of its pronouncement is vouched for by the personality itself, which defies all change. Inclination can only say: that is good *for your individuality* and *for your present need*, but your individuality and your present need will be swept away by change, and what you now ardently desire will one day become the object of your abhorrence. But

66

when the moral feeling says: *this shall be*, it decides for ever and aye—when you acknowledge truth because it is Truth and practise justice because it is Justice, you have turned a single case into a law for all cases, and treated one moment of your life as eternity.

When therefore the formal impulse holds sway, and the pure object acts within us, there is the highest expansion of being, all barriers disappear, and from being the unit of magnitude to which the needy sense confined him, Man has risen to a *unit of idea* embracing the whole realm of phenomena. By this operation we are no more in time, but time, with its complete and infinite succession, is in us. We are no longer individuals, but species; the judgement of all spirits is expressed by our own, the choice of all hearts is represented by our action.

Thirteenth Letter

AT first sight nothing appears more self-contradictory than the tendencies of these two impulses, one aiming at mutation and the other at immutability. And yet it is these two impulses that exhaust the conception of humanity, and a third fundamental impulse, which should reconcile these two, is a quite inconceivable idea. How then are we to restore the unity of human nature, which seems to have been completely destroyed by this primitive and radical opposition?

It is true that their tendencies contradict one another, but—this is the point to be noticed—not in the same objects, and things that do not meet cannot come into collision. The sense impulse indeed demands alteration, but not that it should be extended to the person and its sphere, not any alteration of principles. The form impulse aims at unity and persistence—but it does not require the condition to be stabilized as well as the person, or that there should be identity of sensation. They are, therefore, not by nature mutually opposed, and if nevertheless they appear to be, they have only become so by a willing transgression of Nature, by misunderstanding themselves and confounding their spheres.[1] To watch over these two impulses, and to secure for each its boundaries, is the task of *culture,* which

[1] Once we assert the primary, and therefore necessary, antagonism of the two impulses, there is really no other means of preserving the unity in Man except by the unconditional *subordination* of the sensuous impulse to the rational. But the only result of that is mere uniformity, not harmony, and Man remains for ever divided. Subordination there must indeed be, but it must be reciprocal; for although limits can never establish the Absolute—that is, freedom can never be dependent on time—it is equally certain that the Absolute by itself can never establish the limits, that conditions in time cannot be dependent on freedom. Both principles are therefore at once mutually subordinated and co-ordinated—that is, they act and react upon each other; without form no matter, without matter no form. (This conception of reciprocal action, and its whole importance, we find admirably expounded in Fichte's *Foundation of the Whole Theory of Science,* Leipzig, 1794.) Admittedly we do not know how it fares with the personality in the realm of ideas; but we know for certain that it is unable to manifest itself in the realm of time without recourse to matter; in this realm, then, matter will have something to determine not merely *under* form, but also *alongside* form and independently of it. Necessary as it may be that feeling should decide nothing in the realm of reason, it is equally necessary that reason should not presume to decide anything in the realm of feeling. In the very act of awarding to either of them its own territory we are shutting the other out, and giving each of them a boundary which can be crossed only to the injury of both.

In a transcendental philosophy, where everything depends on freeing form from content and keeping what is necessary clear from everything fortuitous, we too easily become accustomed to think of the material simply as a hindrance, and to represent the sense faculty as necessarily opposed to reason because in this particular matter it stands in our way. Certainly such a mode of thinking is by no means in the *spirit* of the Kantian system, but it may very well be found in the *letter* of it.

therefore owes justice equally to both, and has to uphold not only the rational impulse against the sensuous, but also the latter against the former. Thus its business is twofold: first, to secure the sense faculty against the encroachments of freedom; secondly, to secure the personality against the power of sensation. The former it achieves by the cultivation of the capacity for feeling, the latter by the cultivation of the capacity for reason.

As the world is something extended in time, something that varies, the perfection of that faculty which connects Man with the world will have to possess the highest possible degree of variability and extensity. As personality is the persisting element in the variation, so the perfection of that faculty which is to oppose change will have to possess the highest possible degree of autonomy and intensity. The more multiform the cultivation of the sensibility is, the more variable it is, and the greater the surface it offers to phenomena, the more world does Man *apprehend*, the more potentialities does he develop within himself; the greater the strength and depth that the personality achieves, and the more freedom the reason gains, the more world does Man *comprehend*, the more form does he create outside himself. Thus his culture will consist of two things: first, providing the receptive faculty with the most multifarious contacts with the world, and as regards feeling, pushing passivity to its fullest extent; secondly, securing for the determining faculty the fullest independence from the receptive, and as regards reason, pushing activity to its fullest extent. Where both qualities are united, Man will combine the greatest fullness of existence with the utmost self-dependence and freedom, and instead of abandoning himself to the world he will rather draw it into himself with the whole infinity of its phenomena, and subject it to the unity of his reason.

But Man can *invert* this situation, and thereby fail of his destination in a twofold way. He can lay upon the passive power the intensiveness required by the active, forestall the formal impulse by means of the material, and turn the receptive faculty into a determining one. Or he can assign to the active power the extensiveness which is proper to the passive, forestall the material impulse by means of the formal, and substitute the determining for the receptive faculty. In the first case he never becomes himself, in the second he will never be other than himself; consequently, in both cases he is neither one nor the other, and is therefore—a non-entity.[1]

[1] The bad influence of an overpowering sensuousness upon our thoughts and actions will be easily apparent to everyone; the pernicious influence of an overpowering rationality upon our knowledge and our conduct is not so evident, although it occurs just as frequently and is just as important. Permit me therefore to refer to two only, out of the great quantity of relevant instances, which may serve to illustrate the damage caused by reflection and volition encroaching upon intuition and perception.

One of the chief reasons why our physical sciences make such slow progress is obviously the widespread and almost insurmountable tendency towards teleological judgements, in which, as soon as they are used constitutively, the determining faculty is substituted for the receptive. Nature may touch our organs as vigorously and variously as you please—all her diversity is lost upon us, because we are looking for nothing in her but what we have put there, because we do not allow her to come forward to meet us, from without, but rather strive with impatiently anticipating reason to go out from within ourselves to meet her. And if in the course of centuries one man comes along who approaches her with calm, pure and open senses, and therefore encounters a number of phenomena which we by our anticipation have overlooked, we are mightily astonished that so many eyes in such bright daylight should not have noticed anything. This premature striving for harmony before we have gathered together the separate sounds of which it is to consist, this violent usurpation of the intellectual faculty in a field where its authority is only conditional, is the cause of the sterility of so many thinkers for the greatest benefit of science, and it is hard to say whether sense-faculty which admits of no form, or reason which abides no content, has done the greater harm to the extension of our knowledge.

It is just as hard to decide whether our practical philanthropy is

If then the sense impulse becomes the determining one, if sense is the law-giver, and the world suppresses the personality, the latter loses as object in proportion as it gains as power. As soon as Man is only a content of time, *he* is no longer, and consequently he *has* no content either. His condition is annulled together with his personality, because both are correlative notions—because variation implies something that persists, and finite reality an

more disordered and chilled by the vehemence of our desires or by the rigidity of our principles, more by the egoism of our senses or by the egoism of our reason. In order to make us co-operative, helpful, active people, feeling and character must be united, just as susceptibility of sense must combine with vigour of intellect in order to furnish us with experience. How can we be fair, kindly and humane towards others, let our maxims be as praiseworthy as they may, if we lack the capacity to make strange natures genuinely and truly a part of ourselves, appropriate strange situations, make strange feelings our own? But this capacity, both in the education that we receive and in that which we give ourselves, is stifled in proportion as we seek to break the power of desires and to strengthen the character by means of principles. Because it is difficult to remain true to our principles amidst all the ardour of the feelings, we adopt the more comfortable expedient of making the character more secure by blunting the feelings, for it is certainly infinitely easier to keep calm in the face of an unarmed adversary than to master a spirited and active foe. In this operation, then, consists for the most part what we call the forming of a human being; and that in the best sense of the term, as signifying the cultivation of the inner, not merely the outward, man. A man so formed will indeed be secured against being crude Nature, and from appearing as such; but he will at the same time be armed by his principles against every sensation of Nature, and humanity from without will be as little accessible to him as humanity from within.

We make a most pernicious abuse of the ideal of perfection when we employ it, in all its severity, as the basis of our judgement of other people, and in cases where we should be acting in their interests. The former leads to exaggerated enthusiasm, the latter to harshness and frigidity. Certainly we render our social duties uncommonly easy by mentally substituting for the *actual* man who demands our help, the *ideal* man who could probably help himself. Sternness with oneself, combined with tenderness towards others, is what constitutes the truly excellent character. But mostly the man who is tender towards others is the same towards himself, and the man who is stern with himself is the same with others; it is the most contemptible character which combines tenderness towards self and sternness with others.

infinite. If the form impulse becomes receptive, that is, if thought anticipates sensation and the person is substituted for the world, it loses as subject and autonomous power in proportion as it usurps the place of the object, since permanence implies change and absolute reality some limits for its manifestation. As soon as Man *is* only form, he *has* no form, and his person is extinguished with his condition. In a word, only insofar as he is self-dependent is reality outside him, is he receptive; only insofar as he is receptive is reality within him, is he a thinking power.

Both impulses therefore require restriction and, insofar as they are thought of as energies, moderation; the one, that it may not encroach upon the province of legislation, the other, that it may not invade the realm of sensation. But this moderation of the sense impulse should by no means be the effect of a physical incapacity and a dullness of the perceptions which everywhere merits nothing but contempt; it must be an operation of freedom, an activity of the person, which by its moral intensity mitigates that sensuous intensity, and by controlling the impressions robs them of depth in order to increase their breadth. The character must set bounds to the temperament; for sense must lose only to mind's advantage. Just as little should the moderation of the formal impulse be the effect of an intellectual incapacity and a feebleness of thought and will which would degrade humanity. Fullness of perceptions must be its glorious source; sensation itself must maintain its territory with triumphant power, and resist the violence which by its usurping activity the mind would fain inflict upon it. In a word, the material impulse must be kept by the personality, and the formal impulse by the sensibility, or Nature, each within its proper bounds.

Fourteenth Letter

WE have now reached the conception of a reciprocal action between the two impulses, of such a kind that the operation of the one at the same time confirms and limits the operation of the other, and each one severally reaches its highest manifestation precisely through the activity of the other.

This reciprocal relation of both impulses is, admittedly, a problem of the reason, which Man will be able to solve fully only in the perfection of his being. It is in the truest sense of the term the idea of his humanity, and consequently something infinite to which he can approximate ever nearer in the course of time, without ever reaching it. 'He should not strive for form at the expense of his reality, nor for reality at the expense of form; he should rather seek absolute being through determined being, and determined through infinite being. He should face a world because he is a person, and he should be a person because he is faced by a world. He should feel because he is conscious of himself, and should be conscious of himself because he feels'. He can never learn really to conform to this idea, and consequently to be in the full sense of the word a man, so long as he satisfies only one of these two impulses exclusively, or both only alternately; for so long as he only feels, his personality or his absolute existence remains a mystery to him, and so long as he only thinks, his existence in time or his condition does the same. But if there were cases when he had this twofold experience at the same time, when he was at once conscious of his freedom and sensible of his existence, when he at once felt himself as matter and came to know himself as spirit, he

73

would in such cases, and positively in them alone, have a complete intuition of his humanity, and the object which afforded him this vision would serve him as a symbol of his accomplished destiny, and consequently (since this is only to be attained in the totality of time) as a representation of the Infinite.

Supposing that cases of this sort could actually occur, they would awaken in him a new impulse which, just because the other two work within it, would be opposed to either of them taken in isolation, and would rightly be regarded as a new impulse. The sense impulse requires variation, requires time to have a content; the form impulse requires the extinction of time, and no variation. Therefore the impulse in which both are combined (allow me to call it provisionally the *play impulse*, until I have justified the term), this play impulse would aim at the extinction of time *in time* and the reconciliation of becoming with absolute being, of variation with identity.

The sense impulse wants to *be* determined, to receive its object; the form impulse wants to determine for itself, to produce its object; so the play impulse will endeavour to receive as it would itself have produced, and to produce as the sense aspires to receive.

The sense impulse excludes from its subject all spontaneity and freedom, the form impulse excludes all dependence, all passivity. But exclusion of freedom is physical, while exclusion of passivity is moral, necessity. Both impulses therefore compel the mind, the former through laws of Nature, the latter through laws of Reason. So the play impulse, in which both combine to function, will compel the mind at once morally and physically; it will therefore, since it annuls all mere chance, annul all compulsion also, and set man free both physically and morally. When we embrace with passion someone who deserves our contempt, we feel painfully the compulsion of Nature. When we are unfriendly disposed towards another who commands our respect, we feel painfully the compulsion of Reason. But as soon as a man has at once enlisted our affection and gained our respect, both the constraint of feeling and the constraint of Nature disappear, and we begin to love him—that is, to play at once with our affection and with our respect.

Moreover, since the sense impulse sways us physically and the form impulse morally, the one leaves our formal, and the other our material constitution contingent; that is to say, it is fortuitous whether our happiness agrees with our perfection or the other way about. So the play impulse, in which both operate in combination, will at the same time make our formal and our material constitution, our perfection and our happiness, contingent; it will therefore, just because it makes them both contingent, and because contingency vanishes with necessity, abolish the contingency in them both, and consequently bring form into the material and reality into the form. In proportion as it lessens the dynamic influence of the sensations and emotions, it will bring them in harmony with rational ideas; and in proportion as it deprives the laws of reason of their moral compulsion, it will reconcile them with the interest of the senses.

Fifteenth Letter

I AM drawing ever nearer the goal to which I am leading you, along a not very exhilarating path. If you will consent to follow me a few steps further, a much wider field of view will be displayed, and a cheerful prospect will perhaps reward the exertions of the road.

The object of the sense impulse, expressed in a general concept, may be called *life* in the widest sense of the word; a concept which expresses all material being and all that is immediately present in the senses. The object of the form impulse, expressed generally, may be called *shape*, both in the figurative and in the literal sense; a concept which includes all formal qualities of things and all their relations to the intellectual faculties. The object of the play impulse, conceived in a general notion, can therefore be called *living shape*, a concept which serves to denote all aesthetic qualities of phenomena and—in a word—what we call *Beauty* in the widest sense of the term.

According to this explanation, if it is such, Beauty is neither extended to cover the whole realm of living things, nor merely confined within this realm. A block of marble, therefore, although it is and remains lifeless, can nevertheless become living shape through the architect and sculptor; a human being, although he lives and has shape, is far from being on that account a living shape. That would require his shape to be life, and his life shape. So long as we only think about his shape, it is lifeless, mere abstraction; so long as we only feel his life, it is shapeless, mere impression. Only as the form of something lives in our sensation, and its life takes form in our understanding, is it living shape, and this will everywhere be the case where we judge it to be beautiful.

But by our knowing how to specify the ingredients which combine to produce Beauty, its genesis is by no means yet explained; for that would require that we ourselves grasped that combination which, like all reciprocal action between the finite and the infinite, remains inscrutable to us. Reason demands, on transcendental

76

grounds, that there shall be a partnership between the formal and the material impulse, that is to say a play impulse, because it is only the union of reality with form, of contingency with necessity, of passivity with freedom, that fulfils the conception of humanity. It is obliged to make this demand because it is Reason, because its nature impels it to seek fulfilment and the removal of all barriers, while every exclusive activity of one or other of the impulses leaves human nature unfulfilled and establishes a barrier within it. Consequently, as soon as it issues the command: a humanity shall exist, it has thereby proclaimed the law: there shall be a Beauty. Experience can give us answer *whether* there is a Beauty, and we shall know that as soon as it has taught us whether there is a humanity. But *how* there can be a Beauty, and how a humanity is possible, neither reason nor experience can teach us.

We know that Man is neither exclusively matter nor exclusively spirit. Beauty, therefore, as the consummation of his humanity, can be neither exclusively mere life, as has been maintained by acute observers who adhered too closely to the evidence of experience, a course to which the taste of the age would fain reduce them; nor can it be exclusively mere form, as has been judged by speculative philosophers who strayed too far from experience, and by philosophizing artists who allowed themselves to be influenced overmuch, in their explanation of Beauty, by the requirements of Art;[1] it is the common object of both impulses, that is to say of the play impulse. The term is

[1] Burke, in his *Philosophical Enquiry into the Origin of our Ideas of the Sublime and Beautiful*, turns Beauty into mere life. It is turned into mere form, so far as I am aware, by every adherent of the *dogmatic* system who ever gave testimony upon this subject; among artists, by Raphael Mengs in his *Thoughts on Taste in Painting*. In this department, as in every other, *critical* philosophy has disclosed the way to lead empiricism back to principles and speculation to experience.

77

fully warranted by the usage of speech, which is accustomed to denote by the word play everything that is neither subjectively nor objectively contingent, and yet imposes neither outward nor inward necessity. As our nature finds itself, in the contemplation of the Beautiful, in a happy midway point between law and exigency, so, just because it is divided between the two, it is withdrawn from the constraint of both alike. The material impulse and the formal are equally earnest in their demands, since the former relates in its cognition to the actuality, the latter to the necessity, of things; while in its action the first is directed towards the maintenance of life, the second towards the preservation of dignity—both, that is to say, towards truth and perfection. But life becomes more indifferent as dignity blends with it, and duty compels no longer when inclination begins to attract; in like manner the mind entertains the actuality of things, material truth, more freely and calmly as soon as the latter encounters formal truth, the law of necessity; and it feels itself no longer strained by abstraction as soon as direct contemplation can accompany that truth. In a word, as it comes into association with ideas, everything actual loses its seriousness, because it grows *small*; and as it meets with perception, necessity puts aside its seriousness, because it grows *light*.

But surely, you must long have been tempted to object, surely the Beautiful is degraded by being turned into mere play, and reduced to the level of the frivolous objects which have at all times owned this title? Does it not contradict the rational conception and the dignity of Beauty, which is after all regarded as an instrument of culture, if we limit it to a mere game, and does it not contradict the empirical idea of play, which can co-exist with the exclusion of all taste, to confine it merely to Beauty?

But why call it a *mere* game, when we consider that in every condition of humanity it is precisely play, and play alone, that makes man complete and displays at once his twofold nature? What you call limitation, according to your conception of the matter, I call extension according to mine, which I have justified by proofs. I should therefore prefer to put it in exactly the opposite way: Man is only serious with the agreeable, the good, the perfect; but with Beauty he plays. Certainly we must not here call to mind those games which are in vogue in actual life, and which are commonly concerned only with very material objects; but in actual life we should also seek in vain for the Beauty of which we are now speaking. The Beauty we actually meet with is worthy of the play impulse we actually meet with; but with the ideal of Beauty which Reason sets up, an ideal of the play impulse is also presented which Man should have before him in all his games.

We shall never be wrong in seeking a man's ideal of Beauty along the selfsame path in which he satisfies his play impulse. If the peoples of Greece, in their athletic sports at Olympia, delighted in the bloodless combats of strength, of speed, of agility, and in the nobler combat of talents; and if the Roman people enjoyed the death throes of a vanquished gladiator or of his Libyan antagonist, we can comprehend from this single propensity of theirs why we have to look for the ideal forms of a Venus, a Juno or an Apollo not in Rome but in Greece.[1] But now Reason says:

[1] To confine ourselves to the modern world, if we compare the horse races in London, the bull fights in Madrid, the spectacles of former days in Paris, the gondola races in Venice, the animal baiting in Vienna and the gay, attractive life of the Corso at Rome, it cannot be difficult to differentiate subtly between the tastes of these several peoples. Yet we find among the popular games of the different countries far less uniformity than among the games of the upper classes in these same countries, a fact which is easily accounted for.

the Beautiful is not to be mere life, nor mere shape, but living shape—that is, Beauty—as it dictates to mankind the twofold law of absolute formality and absolute reality. Consequently it also pronounces the sentence: Man shall *only play* with Beauty, and he shall play *only with Beauty*.

For, to declare it once and for all, Man plays only when he is in the full sense of the word a man, and *he is only wholly Man when he is playing*. This proposition, which at the moment perhaps seems paradoxical, will assume great and deep significance when we have once reached the point of applying it to the twofold seriousness of duty and of destiny; it will, I promise you, support the whole fabric of aesthetic art, and the still more difficult art of living. But it is only in science that this statement is unexpected; it has long since been alive and operative in Art, and in the feeling of the Greeks, its most distinguished exponents; only they transferred to Olympus what should have been realized on earth. Guided by its truth, they caused not only the seriousness and the toil which furrow the cheeks of mortals, but also the futile pleasure that smooths the empty face, to vanish from the brows of the blessed gods, and they released these perpetually happy beings from the fetters of every aim, every duty, every care, and made idleness and indifference the enviable portion of divinity; merely a more human name for the freest and sublimest state of being. Not only the material sanction of natural laws, but also the spiritual sanction of moral laws, became lost in their higher conception of necessity, which embraced both worlds at once, and out of the unity of these two necessities they derived true freedom for the first time. Inspired by this spirit, they effaced from the features of their ideal, together with inclination, every trace of volition as well; or rather, they made both unrecognizable because they knew how to unite them both in the closest alliance.

It is neither charm, nor is it dignity, that speaks to us from the superb countenance of a Juno Ludovici; it is neither of them, because it is both at once. While the womanly god demands our veneration, the godlike woman kindles our love; but while we allow ourselves to melt in the celestial loveliness, the celestial self-sufficiency holds us back in awe. The whole form reposes and dwells within itself, a completely closed creation, and—as though it were beyond space—without yielding, without resistance; there is no force to contend with force, no unprotected part where temporality might break in. Irresistibly seized and attracted by the one quality, and held at a distance by the other, we find ourselves at the same time in the condition of utter rest and extreme movement, and the result is that wonderful emotion for which reason has no conception and language no name.

Sixteenth Letter

FROM the interaction of two opposing impulses, then, and from the association of two opposing principles we have seen the origin of the Beautiful, whose highest ideal is therefore to be sought in the most perfect possible union and equilibrium of reality and form. But this equilibrium always remains only an idea, which can never be wholly attained by actuality. In actuality there will always be a preponderance of one element or the other, and the utmost that experience can achieve will consist of an oscillation between the two principles, so that at one moment it is reality, and at another form, that is predominant. Beauty in idea, then, is eternally only something indivisible, unique, since there can exist only one single equilibrium; Beauty in experience, on the other hand, will always be twofold, since through oscillation the balance may be destroyed in a twofold fashion, on one side or the other.

I have observed in one of the foregoing letters, and it may also be necessarily inferred from the connection of all that I have said hitherto, that we may expect from the Beautiful at the same time a relaxing and a tightening effect: a relaxing one, in order to keep not only the sense impulse but also the form impulse within their bounds, a tightening one in order to maintain both of them in their strength. But in idea, these two modes of operation of Beauty should be positively only a single one. It must relax by tightening both natures evenly, and it must tighten by relaxing both natures evenly. This is a natural consequence of the notion of a reciprocal action, in virtue of which both parts jointly condition each other and are conditioned by each other, and the purest product of which is Beauty. But experience affords us no example of any such complete interaction; rather, we invariably find that an overweight gives rise to some deficiency, and a deficiency to some overweight. What, therefore, in the ideally Beautiful is distinguished only in imagination, in the Beautiful of actual experience, in the condition of existence, is really distinct. The ideally Beautiful, although simple and indivisible, reveals in different connections not only a melting but also an energizing quality; in experience a melting and an energizing Beauty do exist. So it is, and so it will be in every case where the absolute is set within the bounds of time, and ideas of the reason have to be realized in humanity. Thus the reflective man conceives of virtue, truth, happiness; but the man of action will only exercise virtues, only apprehend truths, only

enjoy happy days. To lead back these latter to the former
—to achieve instead of moral practices, morality, instead
of things known, knowledge, instead of happy experiences,
happiness, is the business of physical and ethical education; to make Beauty from beautiful objects is the task of
aesthetic education.

Energizing Beauty can no more preserve a man from a
certain residue of savagery and harshness than melting
Beauty can protect him from a certain degree of softness
and enervation. For as the effect of the former is to brace
his nature both in the physical and in the moral sphere,
and to increase its elasticity, it happens all too easily that
the resistance of his temperament and character diminishes
his sensibility to impressions, that his gentler humanity too
suffers a suppression which should affect his crude nature
alone, and that his crude nature experiences an access of
strength which should be available only to his free personality; in periods, therefore, of strength and exuberance we
find real greatness of imagination coupled with the gigantic
and fantastic, and sublimity of feeling with the most
shocking outbursts of passion; while in periods of regu-
larity and of form we find Nature suppressed just as often
as we find her controlled, just as often outraged as surpassed. And since the effect of melting Beauty is to relax
the disposition in the moral as in the physical sphere, it
happens just as easily that with the violence of desire,
energy of feeling too is stifled, and that the character also
shares a diminution of strength which should affect passion
alone; in the so-called ages of refinement, therefore, we
shall see tenderness degenerating not infrequently into
softness, plainness into platitude, correctness into emptiness, liberality into licence, lightness into frivolity, calm-
ness into apathy, and the most despicable caricature side
by side with the most splendid humanity. So melting

Beauty is essential for a man under the constraint either of matter or of form; since he has been moved by greatness and strength long before he began to become sensitive to harmony and grace. The need of a man swayed by the indulgence of taste is for energizing Beauty; since in the state of refinement he fritters away only too lightly a strength which he brought over from the state of savagery.

And now at last, I think, we can explain and answer that contradiction which we usually meet with in the judgements that people make about the influence of the Beautiful, and in their estimation of aesthetic culture. The contradiction is explained as soon as we remember that Beauty is twofold in experience, and that both sides assert of the whole genus what each is only in a position to demonstrate in a particular species of it. The contradiction is resolved the moment we distinguish the twofold need of mankind to which that twofold Beauty corresponds. Both sides will then probably turn out to be right, if only they are first agreed among themselves which kind of Beauty and what form of humanity they have in mind.

In continuing my enquiry I shall therefore pursue the same path which Nature follows with Man in regard to aesthetics, and rise from the species of Beauty to the generic notion of it. I shall examine the effect of melting Beauty on the tense man, and the effect of energizing Beauty on the languid man, in order finally to dissolve both these opposite modes of Beauty in the unity of the ideally Beautiful, just as those two opposite forms of humanity are absorbed in the unity of the ideal man.

Seventeenth Letter

SO long as we were merely engaged in deducing the universal idea of Beauty from the conception of human nature in general, we needed to consider no other boundaries to the latter than those which are directly established in its very being, and are inseparable from the conception of the finite. Unconcerned about the fortuitous limitations which it might suffer in the phenomenal world, we derived our conception of it directly from Reason, as the source of all necessity, and with the ideal of humanity we found at the same time the ideal of Beauty.

But we now descend from the realm of ideas into the arena of actuality, to meet Man in a particular condition, and consequently under limitations which do not originally derive from the mere conception of him, but from external circumstances and from a fortuitous exercise of his freedom. But in however many ways the idea of humanity may be limited in him, we learn from its simple content that in general only two opposite deviations from it can occur. That is to say, if his perfection lies in the harmonious energy of his sensuous and spiritual powers, he can only fall short of this perfection either through a lack of harmony or through a lack of energy. So before we have even heard the testimony of experience concerning it, we are already assured in advance, through sheer reason, that we shall find the actual and therefore limited man either in a condition of tension or in one of relaxation, according as the one-sided activity of isolated powers is disturbing the harmony of his being, or as the unity of his nature is based upon the uniform relaxation of his sensuous and spiritual powers. Both of these opposite limits are, as I shall now shew, removed by means of Beauty, which restores harmony in the tense man and energy in the languid man, and in this way, in accordance with its nature, brings back the condition of limitation to an absolute one and makes of Man a whole, complete in himself.

So Beauty by no means belies in actuality the conception which we formed of her in speculation—only that she has here an incomparably less free hand than when we were considering her in relation to the pure conception of humanity. In Man as experience reveals him she finds a material already vitiated and resistant, which robs her just as much of her ideal perfection as it blends with her by its individual quality. In actuality, therefore, she will everywhere appear only as a particular and limited species, never as a pure genus; she will in taut natures lay aside some of her freedom and diversity, and in relaxed ones some of her invigorating power; but we, who have by now grown more familiar with her true character, shall not be led astray by this contradictory phenomenon. So far from determining our conception of her from isolated experiences, as the great mass of critics do, and making her responsible for the deficiencies which Man reveals under her influence, we know, on the contrary, that it is Man who transfers to her the imperfections of his individuality, who by his subjective limitation perpetually stands in the way of her perfection and reduces her absolute ideal to two limited forms of phenomena.

Melting Beauty, we maintained, was for a taut nature, and energizing Beauty for a relaxed one. But I call a man taut as much when he is under the constraint of sensations as when he is under that of ideas. Every exclusive domination of either of his two fundamental impulses is for him a condition of constraint and of force, and freedom consists solely in the co-operation of both his natures. The man

who is one-sidedly swayed by feelings, or sensuously strait-
ened, is therefore relaxed and set free by form; the man
who is one-sidedly swayed by laws, or spiritually strait-
ened, is relaxed and set free by matter. In order to do
justice to this twofold task, therefore, melting Beauty will
reveal herself in two distinct shapes. Firstly, as quiet form,
she will soften savage life and pave the way for the transition from sensations to thoughts; secondly, as living
shape, she will furnish abstract form with sensuous power,
and lead back conception to contemplation and law to
feeling. The first service she renders to the natural man,
the second to the artificial man. But since in either case she
does not control her material quite freely, but depends on
that which either formless Nature or unnatural Art offers
to her, she will in either case still bear traces of her origin,
and become lost at one point more in material life, at
another more in sheer abstract form.

In order to be able to conceive how Beauty can be a
means of removing that twofold strain, we must seek to
discover her origin in the human disposition. Make up
your mind, therefore, to one further short sojourn in the
region of speculation, in order thereafter to leave it for
ever, to stride forward all the more securely over the fields
of experience.

Eighteenth Letter

THROUGH Beauty the sensuous man is led to form and to
thought; through Beauty the spiritual man is brought back
to matter and restored to the world of sense.

It appears to follow from this that a condition must exist

midway between matter and form, between passivity and activity, and that Beauty transports us into this intermediate condition. This is the conception of Beauty that the majority of people actually form for themselves, as soon as they begin to reflect upon her workings, and all experiences do point that way. But on the other hand nothing is more inconsistent and contradictory than such a conception, since the distance between matter and form, between passivity and activity, between sensation and thought, is infinite, and the two cannot conceivably be reconciled. How are we to remove this contradiction? Beauty combines the two opposite conditions of perceiving and thinking, and yet there is no possible mean between the two of them. The one is made certain through experience, the other directly through reason.

This is the precise point to which the whole question concerning Beauty is leading; and if we succeed in solving this problem satisfactorily we have at the same time the clue which will lead us through the whole labyrinth of aesthetics.

It is really a question of two utterly different operations, which in this enquiry must necessarily support each other. Beauty, it is said, links together two conditions which are *opposed to each other* and can never become one. It is from this opposition that we must start; we must comprehend and recognize it in its whole purity and strictness, so that the two conditions are separated in the most definite way; otherwise we are mixing but not uniting them. Secondly, it is said that Beauty *combines* those two opposite conditions, and thus removes the opposition. But since both conditions remain eternally opposed to one another, they can only be combined by cancellation.[1] Our

[1] The German word thus inadequately translated is *aufgehoben*, which is here used, possibly for the first time, to mean *preserved by*

second business, then, is to make this combination perfect, to accomplish it so purely and completely that both conditions entirely disappear in a third, and no trace of the division remains behind in the whole; otherwise we are isolating but not uniting them. All the disputes that have ever prevailed in the philosophical world, and still prevail to some extent nowadays, about the conception of Beauty, have the single origin that people either began the enquiry without the requisite strictness of discr..nination, or else did not carry it through to a completely pure combination. Those philosophers who blindly trust the guidance of their feelings in considering the subject can arrive at no *concept* of Beauty, because they distinguish nothing individual in the totality of the sensuous impression. The others, who take the intellect as their exclusive guide, can never arrive at a concept of *Beauty*, because they never see in its totality anything but the parts, and spirit and matter remain, even in completest union, for ever separate to them. The first are afraid of invalidating Beauty *dynamically*—that is, as an operative power—by separating what is yet combined in the feeling; the others are afraid of invalidating Beauty *logically*—that is, as a concept—by bringing together what is yet separate in the understanding. The former want to think of Beauty as it operates; the latter want to have it operate as it is thought. Both must therefore miss the truth, the former because they seek to rival infinite Nature with their limited intellectual capacity, the latter because

destruction in the dialectical sense. It was to have a long, important and occasionally sinister career in the history of German philosophy. Goethe, indeed, sometimes uses *Aufhebung* to mean *disappearance in a higher import* in a very similar sense; but the peculiar logical context of this passage makes it probable that it was from these Letters that Hegel derived the characteristic technical term of his philosophical system. This whole Letter reveals a logical clarity of thought and expression, and an understanding of the nature of synthesis, which are not usually to be found in Schiller.—*Trans*.

they are trying to restrict infinite Nature to their own intellectual laws. The first are afraid of robbing Beauty of its freedom by analysing it too closely; the others are afraid of destroying the definiteness of its conception by combining it too boldly. But the former do not reflect that the freedom in which they quite rightly place the essence of Beauty is not lawlessness but harmony of laws, not arbitrariness but the utmost inner necessity; the latter do not reflect that the definiteness which they equally rightly demand of Beauty consists not in the *exclusion of certain realities* but in the *absolute inclusion of them all,* so that it is therefore not restriction but infinity. We shall avoid the rocks upon which they both of them founder if we start from the two elements into which Beauty is divided for the intellect, and then later ascend to the pure aesthetic unity through which she works upon the perceptions, and in which both those conditions completely disappear.[1]

[1] The attentive reader will have observed, in the foregoing comparison, that the sensuous aestheticians, who attach greater importance to the testimony of sensation than to that of ratiocination, are *in practice* less far removed from the truth than their opponents, although they are no match for them *in discernment*; and this is the relationship which we find everywhere between Nature and Science. Nature (sensation) everywhere combines, intellect everywhere separates; but Reason combines again; before he begins to philosophize, therefore, Man is nearer truth than the philosopher who has not yet completed his enquiry. We can consequently, without further examination, declare a philosophical conclusion to be erroneous as soon as it has common observation against it in the actual result; but we are equally justified in holding it in suspicion if it has common observation on its side in the matter of form and method. The latter consideration may console every writer who cannot, as many readers apparently expect him to do, propound a philosophical conclusion in the manner of a fireside chat. The former may reduce to silence anyone who wishes to found new systems at the expense of ordinary common sense.

Nineteenth Letter

WE may distinguish in mankind in general two different conditions of passive and active determinability, and as many conditions of passive and active determination. The explanation of this statement will be the shortest way to our goal.

The condition of the human spirit *before* any determination, the one that is given it through impressions of the senses, is an unlimited capacity for being determined. The boundlessness of space and time is presented to Man's imagination for its free employment, and since *ex hypothesi* nothing in this wide realm of the possible is ordained, and consequently nothing is yet excluded, we may call this condition of indeterminability an *empty infinity*, which is by no means to be confused with an infinite emptiness.

And now his sense is to be touched, and out of the infinite number of possible determinations one single one is to attain actuality. A conception is to arise within him. What in the previous condition of mere determinability was nothing but an empty capacity now becomes an operative power that acquires a content; but at the same time it receives, as operative power, a limit, after being as mere capacity unlimited. So reality is there; but infinity is lost. In order to describe a shape in space, we must *set limits* to infinite space; in order to represent to ourselves an alteration in time, we must *divide* the totality of time. So we arrive at reality only through limitation, at the *positive*, or actually established, only through *negation* or exclusion, at determination only through the surrender of our free determinability.

But no reality would arise to all eternity from mere

exclusion, and no idea would arise to all eternity from mere sense perception, unless there were something there *from which* the exclusion could be made, unless by an absolute act of the mind the negation were related to something positive, and from non-entity some entity arose; this activity of the mind is called judging or thinking, and its result is called *thought*.

Before we determine a position in space, there simply is no space for us; but without absolute space we should never be able to determine a position at all. It is the same with time. Before we have the instant, there simply is no time for us; but without everlasting time we should never have a manifestation of the instant. Thus we arrive, to be sure, at the whole only through the part, at the unlimited only through limitation; but we also arrive at the part only through the whole, at limitation only through the unlimited.

So when it is asserted of the Beautiful, that it paves the way for mankind to a transition from sensation to thought, we are by no means to suppose by this that the Beautiful can fill up the gulf which separates sensation from thought, passivity from activity; this gulf is infinite, and without the intervention of a new and autonomous faculty nothing universal can to all eternity arise from the particular, nothing necessary from the fortuitous. Thought is the immediate operation of this absolute capacity, which must indeed be induced by the senses to declare itself, but in its actual declaration depends so little on sense perception that it rather reveals itself only through opposition to it. The self-dependence with which it acts excludes every outside influence; and it is not insofar as she helps reflection (which contains an obvious contradiction), but only insofar as she secures for the intellectual faculties the freedom to express themselves according to their own laws, that Beauty can become a means of leading Man from matter to form, from perception to principles, from a limited to an absolute existence.

But this presupposes that the freedom of the intellectual faculties can be restricted, which seems to conflict with the idea of an autonomous faculty. Because a faculty which receives from outside nothing but the material of its operation, can be hampered in its operation only by the withdrawal of the material, only negatively, and we misconstrue the nature of a human spirit if we attribute to the sensuous passions the power of positively suppressing the freedom of the mind. Experience certainly affords plenty of examples where the rational powers appear to be suppressed in proportion to the violence of the sensuous powers; but instead of deducing this weakness of mind from the strength of the emotion, we should rather explain this overwhelming strength of emotion by the weakness of the mind; for the senses cannot represent an authority over a man except insofar as the mind has of its own free will neglected to establish itself as such.

But while I seek by means of this explanation to meet one objection, I have, it appears, become involved in another, and have secured the self-dependence of the mind only at the expense of its unity. For how can the mind find in itself at the same time the principles of inactivity and of activity, if it is not itself divided, if it is not in opposition to itself?

At this point we must recall that we are considering the finite, not the infinite mind. The finite mind is that which only becomes active through passivity, only attains the absolute by means of limitations, only works and fashions insofar as it receives material. Such a mind will accordingly associate with the impulse towards form, or towards the absolute, an impulse towards the material, or towards limitation, as being the condition without which it could neither possess nor satisfy the first impulse. To decide how two such opposite tendencies can subsist together side by side in the same being, is a task that might indeed set the metaphysician—though not the transcendental philosopher—in sore perplexity. The latter does not presume to explain the possibility of things, but contents himself with establishing the knowledge from which the possibility of experience is apprehended. And as experience could as little exist without that opposition in the mind, as it could without the mind's absolute unity, he maintains both concepts with complete justification as equally necessary conditions of experience, without troubling himself further about their compatibility. Moreover, this indwelling of two fundamental impulses in no way contradicts the absolute unity of the mind, as soon as we distinguish the latter itself from both the impulses. Certainly each impulse exists and operates within the mind, but the mind itself is neither matter nor form, neither sensuousness nor reason, a fact which does not always seem to have been considered by those who only allow the human mind to be active when it proceeds according to reason, and where it contradicts reason declare it to be merely passive.

Each of these two fundamental impulses, as soon as it has developed, strives by its nature and by necessity towards satisfaction; but just because both are necessary and both are yet striving towards opposite objectives, this twofold constraint naturally cancels itself, and the will preserves complete freedom between them both. It is therefore the will that maintains itself towards both impulses as an authority (as basis of actuality), but neither of the two can of its own accord act as an authority against the other. By the most positive inclination to justice, which he by no means lacks, the violent man is not withheld from injustice, and the strong-minded man is not led to a breach of his principles by the keenest temptation to enjoyment. There is in Man no other authority than his will, and only something that annuls the man himself—death, or some deprivation of his consciousness—can annul his inner freedom.

A necessity *outside ourselves* determines our condition, our existence in time, by means of sense perception. This is quite involuntary, and as it acts upon us so we must abide it. Similarly a necessity *inside ourselves* reveals our personality, at the direction of that sense perception and through opposition to it; for consciousness of self cannot depend upon the will, which presupposes it. This primitive manifestation of the personality is no more a merit than the absence of it is a defect in us. Reason—that is to say absolute consistency and universality of consciousness—is required only from the man who is conscious of himself; before that he is not a man, nor can any act of humanity be expected from him. The *metaphysician* can no more account for the limits which the free and autonomous mind meets with in sensation, than the *physicist* can comprehend the infinity which is revealed in the personality through these limits. Neither abstraction nor experience will lead us back to the source from which our concepts of universality and necessity derive; its early appearance in time hides it from the observer, and its suprasensible origin from the metaphysical enquirer. It is sufficient that the consciousness of self is there, and together with its own unalterable unity the law of unity for everything that is *for* man, and for everything that is to come about *through* him, is established for his apprehension and his activity. Inescapable, incorruptible, inconceivable, the concepts of truth and right present themselves even in the age of sensuousness, and without being able to say whence and how it arose we are aware of the eternal in time and the necessary in the train of chance. So sensation and the consciousness of self arise, entirely without the assistance of the personality, and the origin of them both lies as much beyond our will as it lies beyond the sphere of our knowledge.

But if both are real, and if Man has had by means of sensation the experience of a definite existence, and through apperception the experience of his own absolute existence, both his fundamental impulses will be aroused directly their objects are pr esent. The sensuous impulse awakens with the experience of life (with the beginning of the individual), the rational with the experience of law (with the beginning of the personality), and only at this point, after both of them have come into existence, is his humanity established. Until this has happened, everything in him has proceeded according to the law of necessity; but now Nature's hand abandons him, and it is his own business to assert the humanity which she planned and disclosed in him. As soon, that is to say, as both the opposite fundamental impulses are active in him, they both lose their sanction, and the opposition of two necessities gives rise to *freedom*.[1]

---

[1] To avoid any misconception I would observe that whenever I speak of freedom I do not mean the sort which necessarily attaches to Man in his capacity as intelligent being, and can neither be given to him nor taken from him, but the sort which is based upon his composite nature. By only acting, in general, in a rational manner, Man displays a freedom of the first kind; by acting rationally within the limits of his material and materially within the laws of actuality, he displays a freedom of the second kind. We might explain the latter simply as a natural possibility of the former.

Twentieth Letter

IT follows from the very conception of freedom that it cannot be subject to influence; but that freedom itself is an operation of *Nature* (in the widest sense of the term) and not a work of Man, and can therefore be promoted and hampered by natural means, follows equally necessarily from what has been said. It first arises only when Man is *complete*, and *both* his fundamental impulses have developed; it must therefore be lacking so long as he is incomplete, and one of the two impulses is excluded, and it must be restored by means of everything that gives him back his completeness.

Now it is possible to point to an actual moment, both in the whole race and in the individual human being, in which Man is not yet complete, and one of the two impulses is exclusively active in him. We know that he begins with mere life, in order to end with form; that he is individual before he is a person, that he passes from limitations to infinity. The sense impulse therefore comes into operation earlier than the rational, because sensation precedes consciousness, and in this *priority* of the sense impulse we find the key to the whole history of human freedom.

There is in fact a moment when the impulse to live— since the formal impulse is not yet contradicting it— operates as Nature and as necessity, when sensuousness is an authority, since Man has not yet begun; for in Man himself there can be no authority other than the will. But in the state of reflection to which Man is now to pass over, precisely the opposite is the case—Reason is to be an

97

authority, and a logical or moral necessity is to take the place of the physical. That authority of sensation must therefore be destroyed, before the law that governs it can be established. So it is not enough for something to begin which did not previously exist; something must first cease which previously did exist. Man cannot pass directly from sensation to thought; he must take a step backward, since only by the removal of one determination can the contrary one make its appearance. In order, therefore, to exchange passivity for self-dependence, an inactive determination for an active one, he must be momentarily free from all determination and pass through a condition of mere determinability. Consequently, he must in a certain fashion return to that negative condition of sheer indeterminacy in which he existed before anything at all made an impression upon his sense. But that condition was completely devoid of content, and it is now a question of reconciling an equal indeterminacy and an equally unlimited determinacy with the greatest possible degree of content, since something positive is to result directly from this condition. The determination which he received by means of sensation must therefore be preserved, because he must not lose hold of reality; but at the same time it must, insofar as it is a limitation, be removed, because an unlimited determinacy is to make its appearance. His task is therefore to annihilate and at the same time to preserve the determination of his condition, a thing which can be done in only one way—by opposing that determination with another. The scales of a balance stand level when they are empty; but they also stand level when they contain equal weights.

The mind, then, passes from sensation to thought through a middle disposition in which sensuousness and reason are active *at the same time*, but just because of this they are mutually destroying their determining power and through their opposition producing negation. This middle disposition, in which our nature is constrained neither physically nor morally and yet is active in both ways, pre-eminently deserves to be called a free disposition; and if we call the condition of sensuous determination the physical, and that of rational determination the logical and moral, we must call this condition of real and active determinacy the *aesthetic*.[1]

[1] For readers to whom the pure significance of this word—so often misused through ignorance—is not entirely familiar, what follows may serve as an explanation. Every phenomenon whatsoever may be thought of in four different connections. A thing may relate directly to our sensuous condition (our being and well-being); that is its *physical* character. Or it can relate to our reason, and furnish us with knowledge; that is its *logical* character. Or it can relate to our will, and be regarded as an object of choice for a rational being; that is its *moral* character. Or finally, it can relate to the totality of our various powers, without being a specific object for any single one of them; that is its *aesthetic* character. A man can be pleasant to us through his readiness to oblige; he can cause us to think by means of his transactions; he can instil respect into us by his high moral standards; but finally, independently of all these and without our taking into consideration any law or any design in our own judgement of him, but simply contemplating him, simply by his manifesting himself—he can please us. In this last-named character we are judging him aesthetically. So there is an education for health, an education for understanding, an education for morality, and an education for taste and for Beauty. This last has as its aim the cultivation of the whole of our sensuous and intellectual powers in the fullest possible harmony. But because people are meanwhile led astray by a false taste, and still more confirmed in this error by false reasoning, into taking the conception of arbitrariness along with them into the conception of the aesthetic, I add this superfluous note (though these letters about aesthetic education are concerned with practically nothing else but a refutation of that error) to point out that the mind in its aesthetic condition, although it certainly acts freely and is in the highest degree free from all restraint, is by no means free from laws, and that this aesthetic freedom is to be distinguished from the logical necessity of thinking and from the moral necessity of willing only by the fact that the laws which guide the operation of the mind are not realized, and because they meet with no resistance do not appear as compulsion.

Twenty-first Letter

THERE is, as I observed at the beginning of the previous letter, a twofold condition of determinacy, and a two-fold condition of determination. I can now clarify this statement.

The mind is determinable merely insofar as it is not determined at all; but it is also determinable insofar as it is not determined exclusively—that is to say, is not limited in its determination. The former is mere indeterminacy (it is without limits because it is without reality); the latter is the aesthetic determinacy (it has no limits because it combines all reality).

The mind is determined insofar as it is limited at all; but it is also determined insofar as it limits itself of its own absolute capacity. It finds itself in the first situation when it perceives, in the second when it reflects. So what reflection is in regard to determination, that the aesthetic disposition is in regard to determinacy; the former is limitation proceeding from an infinite inner power, the latter is negation resulting from an infinite inner abundance. Just as sensation and thought have one single point of contact with each other, that in both conditions the mind is determining, that Man is exclusively something—either individual or person—but otherwise are to all eternity separated from each other; so aesthetic determinacy has one single point in common with mere indeterminacy, that both of them exclude every determined existence, while in all other points they are as everything and nothing, and are therefore eternally different. If then the latter, determinacy arising from deficiency, was conceived as an *empty infinity*, aesthetic freedom of determination, which is its proper counterpart, must be regarded as a *filled infinity*, an idea which coincides exactly with the teachings of the foregoing enquiry.

In the aesthetic condition, then, Man is a *cipher*, insofar as we are considering an isolated result and not the whole capacity, and are regarding the absence of any particular determination inside him. We must therefore acknowledge those people to be entirely right who declare the Beautiful, and the mood into which it transports our spirit, to be wholly indifferent and sterile in relation to *knowledge* and *mental outlook*. They are entirely right; for Beauty gives no individual result whatever, either for the intellect or for the will; it realizes no individual purpose, either intellectual or moral; it discovers no individual truth, helps us to perform no individual duty,[1] and is, in a word, equally incapable of establishing the character and clearing the mind. A man's personal worth or dignity, then, insofar as this can depend upon himself, remains completely undetermined by aesthetic culture, and nothing more has been accomplished except that it has been rendered possible for him *on the part of Nature* to make of himself what he chooses— that he has had completely restored to him the freedom to be what he ought to be.

But precisely by this means something infinite is attained. For as soon as we recall that it was this very freedom which was taken from him by the one-sided constraint of Nature in his perception and by the preclusive legislation of Reason in his thinking, we must regard the faculty which is restored to him in the aesthetic disposition as the highest of all gifts, as the gift of humanity. Certainly he already possesses this humanity as a predisposition, before any definite condition

---

[1] This was the passage that aroused Ruskin's indignation in the Third Part of *Modern Painters*, and was characterized by him as 'that gross and inconceivable falsehood' (Sec. 1, chap. 15, § 9); but he cannot have read the remark in its full and proper context.—*Trans.*

into which he may come; but in actual practice he loses it with every definite condition into which he comes, and it must, if he is to be able to make the transition to an opposite condition, be newly restored to him every time by means of the aesthetic life.[1]

It is then no mere poetic licence, but also philosophical truth, to call Beauty our second creator. For although she only makes humanity possible for us, and for the rest leaves it to our own free will to what extent we wish to make it actual, she has this in common with our original creator Nature, who similarly conferred on us nothing beyond the capacity for humanity, but left its exercise to our own volition.

Twenty-second Letter

IF therefore the aesthetic disposition of the mind must be regarded in one sense as a *cipher*—as soon, that is, as we confine our attention to individual and definite operations —yet in another respect it is to be looked upon as a con-

---

[1] Admittedly the speed with which certain characters pass from sensations to thoughts and to resolutions allows the aesthetic temper which they must necessarily hurry through in this time to be barely, if at all, perceptible. Such natures cannot long tolerate the condition of indeterminacy, and press impatiently for a result which they do not find in the condition of aesthetic boundlessness. With others, on the other hand, who find their enjoyment more in the feeling of the *whole faculty* rather than any *individual* action of it, the aesthetic condition displays itself over a much wider surface. As much as the former fear vacuity, so little are the latter able to bear limitation. I need hardly mention that the former are born for detail and for subordinate occupations, the latter—supposing that they also combine reality with this faculty of theirs—for the community and for distinguished rôles in life.

dition of the *highest reality*, insofar as we are considering the absence of all limits and the sum total of the powers which are jointly engaged within it. We can therefore as little declare those people to be wrong who maintain that the whole aesthetic condition is the most fruitful in relation to knowledge and morality. They are entirely right; for a disposition which comprises in itself the wholeness of humanity must necessarily include every individual expression of it according to its capacity; a disposition which removes all limits from the totality of human nature must necessarily remove them also from every individual expression of it. Precisely because it takes no individual function of humanity exclusively under its protection, it is well disposed to every one of them without distinction, and it favours no single one especially, just because it is the ground of the possibility of them all. Every other exercise gives the mind some particular aptitude, but also sets it in return a particular limitation; the aesthetic alone leads to the unlimited. Every other condition into which we can come refers us to some previous one, and requires for its solution some other condition; the aesthetic alone is a whole in itself, as it combines in itself all the conditions of its origin and of its continued existence. Here alone do we feel ourselves snatched outside time, and our humanity expresses itself with a purity and integrity as though it had not yet experienced any detriment from the influence of external forces.

What flatters our sense in immediate perception opens our soft and sensitive nature to every impression, but it also makes us in the same measure less capable of exertion. What braces our intellectual powers and invites us to abstract concepts, strengthens our mind for every kind of resistance, but also hardens it proportionately, and deprives us of sensibility just as much as it helps us towards a greater spontaneity. For that very reason the one, no less than the other, finally leads inevitably to exhaustion, since the material cannot long go without the formative force, nor the formative force long dispense with the plastic material. On the other hand, when we have abandoned ourselves to the enjoyment of genuine Beauty, we are at such a moment masters in equal degree of our passive and our active powers, and shall turn with equal facility to seriousness or to play, to rest or to movement, to compliance or to resistance, to abstract thinking or to beholding.

This lofty serenity and freedom of the spirit, combined with strength and vigour, is the mood in which a genuine work of art should leave us, and there is no surer touchstone of true aesthetic excellence. If we find ourselves after an enjoyment of this kind especially disposed towards some particular mode of feeling or of action, and unfitted and unworthy for another, this serves as an infallible proof that we have experienced no purely aesthetic effect, whether owing to the object or to our mode of perception or (as is almost always the case) to both together.

As in actuality no purely aesthetic effect is to be met with (for Man can never step outside the dependence of his powers), the excellence of a work of art can consist only in the closeness of its approximation to that ideal of aesthetic purity; and with all the freedom with which we may enhance it, we shall always leave it in a particular mood and with a specific tendency. The more universal the mood, and the less limited the tendency which is given to our nature by a definite type of art and by a definite product of the same, the nobler that type is and the more excellent will such a product be. We can test this with works taken from different arts, and with works of each several art. We leave a beautiful piece of music with lively feelings, a beautiful poem with quickened imagination, a beautiful statue or building with awakened understanding; but anyone who sought to invite us immediately after deep musical enjoyment to abstract thought, to employ us immediately after a deep poetic enjoyment in some formal business of everyday life, to inflame our imagination or to surprise our feelings immediately after a contemplation of beautiful paintings and sculpture, would not be choosing his moment well. The reason is that even the most etherial music, by reason of its matter, has a closer affinity with the senses than true aesthetic freedom allows; that even the happiest poem still has a greater share of the arbitrary and fortuitous play of imagination, which is its medium, than the inner necessity of the truly Beautiful permits; that even the most admirable piece of sculpture—and this perhaps most of all—borders on severe science by reason of the positiveness of its conception. These special affinities, however, are lost in proportion as a work of one of these types of art attains a higher level, and it is a necessary and natural consequence of their perfection that, without shifting their objective limits, the various arts are becoming increasingly similar to each other in their effect upon our natures. Music in its loftiest exaltation must become shape, and act upon us with the tranquil power of the antique; the plastic and graphic arts must become music, and move us through their immediate sensuous presence; poetry in its most perfect development must, like musical art, take powerful hold of us, but at the same time, like plastic art, surround us with quiet clarity. It is just in this that perfect style in any art reveals itself—that it is capable of removing the characteristic limitations of that art, without however removing its specific excellences, and of lending it a more universal character by a wise employment of its idiosyncrasy.

105

And the artist must not only overcome, by his treatment, the limitations which are inherent in the specific character of his type of art, but also those belonging to the particular material with which he is dealing. In a truly beautiful work of art the content should do nothing, the form everything; for the wholeness of Man is affected by the form alone, and only individual powers by the content. However sublime and comprehensive it may be, the content always has a restrictive action upon the spirit, and only from the form is true aesthetic freedom to be expected. Therefore, the real artistic secret of the master consists in his *annihilating the material by means of the form,* and the more imposing, arrogant and alluring the material is in itself, the more autocratically it obtrudes itself in its operation, and the more inclined the beholder is to engage immediately with the material, the more triumphant is the art which forces back material and asserts its mastery over form. The nature of the man who sees or hears the work must remain completely free and inviolate, it must go forth from the magic circle of the artist pure and perfect as from the Creator's hands. The most frivolous subject must be so treated that we remain disposed to pass over immediately from it to the strictest seriousness. The most serious material must so be treated that we retain the capability of exchanging it immediately for the lightest play. The arts of emotion, such as tragedy, are no exception; for in the first place they are not entirely free arts, since they are enlisted in the service of a particular aim (that of pathos), and then too no real connoisseur will be likely to deny that works, even of this class, are all the more perfect according as they respect the freedom of the spirit even in the greatest storm of the emotions. There is a fine art of passion, but an impassioned fine art is a contradiction in terms; for the inevitable effect of the Beautiful is freedom from passions.

No less self-contradictory is the notion of a fine instructive (didactic) or improving (moral) art, for nothing is more at variance with the concept of Beauty than that it should have a tendentious effect upon the character.

Nevertheless it does not always argue formlessness in a work, if it makes its effect solely through its content; it can just as often be evidence of a lack of form in the observer. If he is either too tense or too languid, if he is accustomed to read either with his intellect alone or with his senses alone, he will get no further than the parts even with the most felicitous whole, and no further than the matter even with the most beautiful form. Being responsive only to the crude element, he must first shatter the aesthetic organization of a work before he finds enjoyment in it, and carefully disinter the particular qualities which the master with infinite art has caused to vanish in the harmony of the whole. His interest in it is either solely moral or solely physical; only precisely what it ought to be—aesthetic—it is not. Readers of this kind will enjoy a serious and pathetic poem like a sermon, and a naive or droll one like an intoxicating draught; and if they were sufficiently lacking in taste to demand edification from a tragedy or an epic—even if it were a *Messiah* [1]—they will not fail to be scandalized by a song in the manner of Anacreon or Catullus.

Twenty-third Letter

I TAKE up the thread of my enquiry again, which I have only broken off in order to apply the principles laid down

---

[1] Epic poem by Klopstock (1724–1803).—*Trans.*

above to practical art and to the appreciation of its works. The transition from the passive condition of perceiving to the active one of thinking and willing is only effected, then, through an intermediate condition of aesthetic freedom, and although this condition in itself decides nothing in respect to our judgement or our opinions, and consequently leaves our intellectual and moral values completely problematical, it is yet the necessary condition by which alone we can attain to a judgement and to an opinion. In a word, there is no other way to make the sensuous man rational than by first making him aesthetic.

But, you may object, ought this mediation to be absolutely indispensable? Ought not truth and duty, simply for themselves alone and through themselves, to be able to find an entrance into the sensuous man? To this I must reply that they not only can, but positively should owe their determining power to themselves alone, and nothing would be more at variance with my previous assertions than that they should give the appearance of supporting the opposite opinion. It has been explicitly proved that Beauty offers no interference either to the intellect or to the will, that it interferes with no business either of reflection or of resolution, that it confers on both merely the capacity, but determines absolutely nothing concerning the actual use of this capacity. Here all external help disappears, and the pure logical form—the concept—must speak directly to the intellect, the pure moral form—law—directly to the will.

But that it can do this at all, that there should be only one pure form for the sensuous man—this, I maintain, must first be made possible by the aesthetic temper of our nature. Truth is not something that can be received from outside, like the actuality or the sensuous existence of things; it is something that the intellectual faculty produces spontaneously, in its freedom, and it is just this spontaneity, this freedom that we do not find in the sensuous man. The sensuous man is already determined (physically), and has consequently no longer any free determinacy; this lost determinacy he must necessarily first recover before he can exchange the passive determination for an active one. But he cannot recover it except by losing the passive determination which he had before, or by containing already within himself the active one to which he must pass over. If he merely lost the passive determination, he would at the same time lose also the possibility of an active one, since thought needs a body and form can only be realized in some material. He will therefore contain the other already within himself, he will be determined at the same time passively and actively—that is to say, he will have to become aesthetic.

Through the aesthetic temper, then, the spontaneity of the reason is already revealed in the sphere of sense, the power of perception is already broken within its own boundaries, and the physical man is so far ennobled that the intellectual man now merely requires to be developed from him according to the laws of freedom. Hence the transition from the aesthetic condition to the logical and moral (from Beauty to truth and duty) is infinitely easier than the transition from the physical condition to the aesthetic (from mere blind life to form). The former step a man can achieve through his sheer freedom, since he only needs to take and not to give himself, only to separate the elements of his nature, not to enlarge it; the aesthetic-ally-determined man will judge and act with universal validity as soon as he wishes to. The transition from crude matter to Beauty, where an entirely new activity is to be revealed in him, must be facilitated for him by Nature, and his will can dictate nothing concerning a mood which itself gives its very existence to that will. In order to lead the aesthetic man to knowledge and lofty sentiments, we have only to give him serious motives; in order to achieve as much for the sensuous man we must first alter his nature. With the former, it often needs nothing but the challenge of a sublime situation (which acts most directly upon the volitional faculty) in order to make a hero or a sage of him; the latter needs to be first transported to another climate.

It is therefore one of the most important tasks of culture to subject Man to form even in his purely physical life, and to make him aesthetic as far as ever the realm of Beauty can extend, since the moral condition can be developed only from the aesthetic, not from the physical condition. If Man is to possess in each individual case the faculty of making his judgement and his will the judgement of the human species, if from every limited existence he is to find the way through to an infinite one, out of every dependent condition to be able to make the leap forward to self-dependence and freedom, he must take care not to be at any moment merely individual, serving merely the natural law. If he is to be ready and able to rise out of the narrow circle of natural ends to rational ends, he must already have practised himself for the latter while he was within the former, and have already realized his physical determination with a certain freedom that belongs to spiritual nature—that is, according to laws of Beauty.

And certainly he can do this without thereby in the least acting counter to his physical aim. Nature's claims upon him are concerned merely with *what* he does, with the contents of his action; about the *way* in which he works, about its form, nothing is determined by natural ends. The claims of Reason, on the other hand, are directed strictly towards the form of his activity. Necessary as it is, therefore, for his moral determination that he should be purely moral, that he should display an absolute spontaneity, it is a matter of indifference for his physical determination whether he is purely physical, whether he behaves with absolute passivity. In regard to this latter, it is therefore left entirely to his own discretion whether he will exercise it simply as a sentient being and as natural force (as a force, that is, which only acts according as it is acted upon), or at the same time as absolute force, as rational being; and there should be no question which of the two is more in keeping with his dignity. Nay, it humiliates and dishonours him to do something from sensuous motives which he ought to have decided on from pure motives of duty, as much as it dignifies and exalts him to strive for conformity to law, for harmony, for absoluteness, when the common man only satisfies his legitimate craving.[1] In a word, in the realm of truth and morality

[1] This genial and aesthetically free treatment of everyday actuality is, when we come across it, the sign of a *noble* soul. In general, a nature may be called noble which possesses the gift of transforming, by its method of handling it, even the most limited matter and the pettiest object into an infinite one. Every form may be termed noble which impresses the stamp of self-dependence upon something which by its nature merely *subserves* some purpose (is merely a means). A noble spirit is not satisfied with being itself free; it must set free everything around it, even what is lifeless. But Beauty is the only possible expression of freedom in phenomena. The prevailing expression of intellect in a face, in a work of art, and the like, can therefore never prove noble, neither is it ever beautiful, because it emphasizes dependence (which is indistinguishable from conformity to purpose) instead of concealing it.

The moral philosopher indeed teaches us that we can never do *more* than our duty, and he is entirely right if he is referring simply to the relation which actions have to the moral law. But in the case of actions which merely relate to a purpose, to pass *beyond this purpose* into the suprasensible (which must here simply amount to exercising the physical aesthetically) is the same thing as passing *beyond duty*, since the latter can only direct that the *will* shall be holy, not that *Nature* too shall already have hallowed itself. There is, then, admittedly, no moral exceeding of duty, but there is an

sensation must have nothing to determine; but in the sphere of happiness form may exist and the play impulse may govern.

Here already, then, on the neutral field of physical life, Man must start his moral life; even in his state of passivity he must begin his spontaneity, even within his sensuous limits his rational freedom. He must already be imposing the law of his will upon his inclinations; he must, if you will permit me the expression, play at being at war with matter within the boundaries of matter, so that he may be relieved from fighting against this dreadful foe upon the sacred soil of freedom; he must learn to desire more *nobly*, that he may not be compelled to will *sublimely*. This is accomplished by aesthetic culture, which subjects to laws of Beauty everything in which neither natural nor rational laws bind Man's free choice, and in the form which it gives to the outward reveals the inner life.

aesthetic one; and such conduct is called noble. But precisely because in the case of the noble man we are always aware of an excess, in that something which needed to have only a material value now possesses a free, formal value also; or in that it combines with the internal value which it should possess an external value also, which it should be without—many people have confused aesthetic excess with moral, and, led astray by the appearance of what is noble, have introduced a lawlessness and contingency into morality itself, whereby it would be completely cancelled. We should distinguish noble from sublime conduct. The first passes right beyond moral obligation, but not so the second, although we esteem it as far loftier than the other. But we esteem it not because it surpasses the rational notion of its object (the moral law), but because it surpasses the inductive notion of its subject (our knowledge of human goodness of will); so inversely, we value noble conduct not because it transcends the nature of its subject, from which it must rather flow with complete unconstraint, but because it passes beyond the nature of its object (the physical aim) into the realm of spirit. In the first case, it might be said, we are astonished at the victory which the object wins over Man; in the second, we marvel at the impetus which Man gives to the object.

Twenty-fourth Letter

WE may distinguish, then, three separate moments or stages of development, which not only the individual man but also the whole race must pass through, and in a particular order, if they are to complete the whole circle of their determination. For accidental reasons, which lie either in the influence of external things or in the free choice of Man, the several periods can certainly be now lengthened and now shortened, but none can be entirely passed over, and even the order in which they follow one another cannot be reversed either by Nature or by the will. Man in his *physical* condition is subject to the power of Nature alone; he shakes off this power in the *aesthetic*, and he controls it in the *moral* condition.

What is Man before Beauty lures from him his free enjoyment and tranquil form tempers his wild life? Eternally uniform in his aims, eternally shifting in his judgements, self-seeking without being himself, unfettered without being free, a slave though serving no rule. At this period the world to him is merely destiny, not yet object; everything has existence for him only insofar as it secures existence for him; what neither gives to him nor takes from him, is to him simply not there. Every phenomenon stands before him single and isolated, just as he finds himself in the ranks of beings. Everything that is, is tó him through the instant's word of command; every change is for him an entirely fresh creation, since together with the necessity *within himself* he lacks that necessity *outside himself* which binds together the varying shapes into a universe, and, with the passing of the individual, holds law firmly upon the scene of action. In vain does Nature allow her rich diversity to pass before his senses; he sees in her splendid profusion nothing but his prey, in her power and greatness nothing but his foe. Either he hurls himself at objects and wants to snatch them into himself in desire; or else the objects force their way destructively into him, and he thrusts them from him in abhorrence. In both cases his relation to the sensible world is immediate contact, and being for ever harassed by its pressure, restlessly tormented by imperious need, he finds rest nowhere but in exhaustion, and limits nowhere but in spent desire.

> *The Titan's mighty breast and nervous frame*
> *His certain heritage . . .*
> *But round his brow Zeus forged a brazen band;*
> *Wisdom and counsel, patience, moderation*
> *It hid before his fearful, sullen glance.*
> *In him each passion grows to savage rage,*
> *Rushes headlong, its violence unchecked.*
>
> IPHIGENIA IN TAURIS [1]

Ignorant of his *own* human dignity, he is far removed from honouring it in others, and conscious of his own savage greed, he fears it in every creature that resembles him. He never perceives others in himself, only himself in others; and society, instead of expanding him into the species, only confines him ever more closely inside his individuality. In this dull limitation he wanders through his twilit life, until a kindly Nature rolls away the burden of matter from his darkened senses, thought distinguishes *himself* from things, and objects at length reveal themselves in the reflection of his consciousness.

This condition of crude Nature, as it has here been depicted, cannot indeed be identified in any particular people or age; it is only an idea, but an idea with which

[1] Slightly altered by Schiller from a passage in Act I, Scene 3 of Goethe's play.—*Trans.*

experience in individual characteristics very closely agrees. Man, we may say, was never quite in this bestial condition, but he has never quite escaped from it. Even in the roughest persons we find unmistakable traces of the free action of reason, just as moments are not absent in the most cultivated which recall that dismal natural state. It is in fact peculiar to Man to combine the highest and the lowest in his nature, and if his *dignity* depends upon a rigid distinction between the two, his *happiness* depends upon a skilful removal of the distinction. So culture, which is to reconcile his dignity with his happiness, will have to provide for the utmost purity of both these principles in their most intimate combination.

The first appearance of reason in Man is, therefore, not yet the beginning of his humanity. The latter is not decided until he is free, and Reason's first serious act is to make his sensuous dependence unlimited—a phenomenon that seems to me to have been insufficiently elucidated so far, considering its importance and universality. Reason, we know, may be recognized in Man by the demand for the absolute (what is based upon, and necessary for, itself alone), which, as it cannot be satisfied in any single condition of his physical life, constrains him to leave the physical altogether and to rise from limited actuality to ideas. But although the true purport of that demand is to tear him away from the limitations of time and to lead him up from the sensuous world to a world of ideas, yet it can through a misconception (one that is scarcely to be avoided in this age of prevailing sensuousness) be directed towards the physical life, and instead of making Man independent it can plunge him into the most fearful servitude.

And thus it happens in practice. On the wings of imagination Man leaves the narrow bounds of the present, in which mere animality is enclosed, in order to strive forward to an unbounded future; but while the infinite rises before his dazed imagination, his heart has not yet ceased to live in the particular and to wait upon the instant. In the midst of his animality the impulse towards the absolute takes him by surprise—and as in this dull condition all his endeavours are directed towards the material and temporal, and are confined solely to his individuality, he is merely induced by that demand, instead of abandoning his individuality, to extend it into the infinite; instead of form, to strive for inexhaustible matter, instead of the immutable for eternal variation and an absolute assertion of his temporal existence. The very impulse which, applied to his thoughts and actions, ought to lead him to truth and morality, now brought to bear on his passivity and perception, produces nothing but a limitless demand, an absolute want. The first fruits which he reaps in the realm of ideas, then, are *care* and *fear*, both of them the effects of reason, not of sensuousness—but of a reason which mistakes its object and applies its imperative directly to the material. Among the fruits of this tree are all unconditional systems of happiness, whether they have the present day or the whole of life, or—what does not make them in the slightest degree more awe-inspiring—the whole of eternity for their object. An infinite perpetuation of being and well-being, merely for the sake of being and well-being, is merely an ideal of appetite, and consequently a demand which can be put forward only by an animality that is striving after the absolute. Without, then, gaining anything for his humanity by a rational expression of this kind, Man only loses thereby the happy limitation of the animal, over which he now possesses merely the unenviable superiority of losing possession of the present as he aspires to the remote, yet without ever seeking in the whole limitless distance anything except the present.

But even if Reason does not mistake its object, or go astray in its questioning, sensuousness will falsify the answer for a long time yet. As soon as Man has begun to use his intellect and to connect the phenomena around him according to causes and effects, Reason presses, in conformity with its conception, for an absolute connection and an unconditioned cause. Simply in order to be able to make such a demand, Man must already have passed beyond sensuousness; but sensuousness makes use of this very demand in order to recall the fugitive. Here, in fact, would be the point where he must leave the world of sense completely, and soar upwards to the realm of pure ideas; for the intellect remains for ever stationed within the conditioned, and for ever goes on asking without ever reaching any finality. But as the man we are here discussing is not yet capable of such abstraction, if he does not find something in his *sphere of sensuous perception,* and does not look above that into pure reason, he will look beneath it in the *sphere of his feelings,* and will only seemingly find it there. Sensuousness, indeed, shews him nothing which could be its own cause or a law for itself, but it shews him something which knows of no cause and respects no law. As therefore he can bring his questioning intellect to rest through no final and inner cause, he at least reduces it to silence through the concept of causelessness, and he remains within the blind compulsion of matter, as he is not yet capable of comprehending the sublime necessity of reason. Since sensuousness knows no other aim but its own advantage, and feels itself impelled by no other cause but blind chance, he makes sensuousness the arbiter of his actions and chance the sovereign of his world.

Even that sacred thing in Man, the moral law, cannot on its first appearance in the sensual world escape this perversion. As it speaks only to forbid, and against the interests of his sensuous self-love, it must appear to him as something alien until he has reached the point of regarding that self-love as the alien thing, and the voice of Reason as his true self. He therefore perceives only the fetters which Reason lays upon him, not the infinite freedom which it procures for him. All unconscious of the dignity of the lawgiver within himself, he perceives only the constraint and the powerless resistance of the submissive subject. Since the sensuous impulse *precedes* the moral in his experience, he gives to the law of necessity a beginning in time, a *positive origin*, and through the most unfortunate of all errors he turns what is changeless and eternal in himself into an accident of transience. He persuades himself into regarding the concepts of right and wrong as statutes ordained by a will, not as things valid in themselves and to all eternity. As he passes beyond *Nature* in explanation of particular natural phenomena, and seeks outside her for what can be found only in her innermost conformity to law, so he passes beyond *Reason* in explanation of morality, and forfeits humanity by seeking a divinity along this road. No wonder that a religion which was acquired at the cost of the abandonment of his humanity shews itself worthy of such an origin, that he considers laws which have not been binding *from* all eternity not to be unconditional and binding *to* all eternity. He is dealing not with a holy, but merely with a powerful, Being. The spirit in which he worships God is therefore fear, which degrades him, not reverence, which exalts him in his own estimation.

Although these various aberrations of Man from the ideal of his determining cannot all take place in the self-same era, seeing that he has to pass through several stages from absence of thought to error, from complete absence of will to depravity of will, yet they are all consequences attendant on the physical condition, since in all of them

118

the impulse to live domineers over the formal impulse. Whether Reason has not yet spoken at all in Man, and the physical still governs him with blind necessity, or whether Reason has not yet purified itself sufficiently from the senses, and the moral is still subservient to the physical, in either case the sole authoritative principle in him is a material one, and Man—at least in his ultimate tendency—is a sensuous being; with the single difference that in the first case he is a non-rational, in the second a rational, animal. But he should be neither of these, he should be a human being; Nature should not rule him exclusively, nor Reason conditionally. Both systems of law should subsist in complete independence, yet in complete accord with one another.

Twenty-fifth Letter

so long as Man in his first physical condition accepts the world of sense merely passively, merely perceives, he is still completely identified with it, and just because he himself is simply world, there is no world yet for him. Not until he sets it outside himself or *contemplates* it, in his aesthetic status, does his personality become distinct from it, and a world appears to him because he has ceased to identify himself with it.[1]

[1] I recall once more that both these periods, though they are indeed necessarily to be distinguished from each other in idea, are in experience more or less intermingled. We are also not to think that there has ever been a time when Man has been situated only in this physical status, or a time when he has shaken himself quite free from it. As soon as a man *sees an object*, he is already no longer in a merely physical condition, and so long as he continues to see an object, he will also not escape from that physical situation, since he can only see insofar as he

Contemplation (reflection) is Man's first free relation to the universe which surrounds him. If desire directly apprehends its object, contemplation thrusts its object into the distance, thereby turning it into its true and inalienable possession and thus securing it from passion. The necessity of Nature which governed him with undivided power in the condition of mere sensation, abandons him when reflection begins; an instantaneous calm ensues in the senses; time itself, the eternally moving, stands still while the dispersed rays of consciousness are gathered together, and *form*, an image of the infinite, is reflected upon the transient foundation. As soon as it becomes light inside Man, there is also no longer any night outside him; as soon as it is calm within him, the storm in the universe is also lulled, and the contending forces of Nature find rest between abiding boundaries. No wonder, therefore, that ancient poetry tells of this great occurrence in the inner Man as of a revolution in the world outside him, and embodies the thought which triumphs over the laws of time in the figure of Zeus who brings the reign of Saturn to an end.

From being a slave of Nature, so long as he merely perceives her, Man becomes her lawgiver as soon as she becomes his thought. She who had formerly ruled him only as *force*, now stands as *object* before the judgement of his glance. What is object to him has no longer power over him; for in order to be object it must experience his own power. Insofar as he gives form to matter, and so long as he gives it, he is invulnerable to her influences; for nothing

perceives. Those three moments, therefore, which I specified at the beginning of my twenty-fourth letter are indeed, regarded in general, three different ages for the development of a whole humanity and for the whole development of individual man, but they may also be distinguished in every particular awareness of an object, and they are, in a word, the necessary conditions of every cognition which we receive through the senses.

can injure a spirit except what deprives it of freedom, and Man proves his freedom by his very forming of the formless. Only where substance holds its ponderous and shapeless sway, and the dim outlines fluctuate between uncertain boundaries, does fear have its abode; Man is superior to every terror of Nature so long as he knows how to give form to it, and to turn it into his object. Just as he begins to assert his self-dependence in the face of Nature as phenomenon, so he also asserts his dignity in the face of Nature as power, and with noble freedom he rises up against his deities. They throw off the ghastly masks with which they had frightened his infancy, and in becoming his own conception they surprise him with his own image. The divine monster of the Oriental, that governs the world with the blind strength of a beast of prey, dwindles in the Grecian fantasy into the friendly outlines of humanity; the empire of the Titans falls, and infinite force is mastered by infinite form.

But while I have been merely looking for a way out of the material world and a passage into the world of spirit, the free range of my imagination has already led me into the midst of the latter. The Beauty that we seek lies already behind us, and we have leapt over her as we passed directly from mere life to pure shape and to pure object. Such a leap is not in human nature, and to keep pace with it we shall have to return to the world of sense.

Beauty is, to be sure, the work of free contemplation, and we step with her into the world of ideas—but, it must be observed, without thereby leaving the world of sense, as is the case with cognition of truth. This latter is the pure product of abstraction from everything that is material and contingent, pure object in which no barrier of subjectivity may remain behind, pure spontaneity without any admixture of passivity. There is, certainly, a way back to sense even from the utmost abstraction; for thought stirs the inner sensation, and the conception of logical and moral unity passes into a feeling of sensuous accord. But when we take delight in cognition, we distinguish very precisely our conception from our sensation, and look upon the latter as something accidental which might very well be omitted without the cognition thereby vanishing, or truth not being truth. But it would be a wholly fruitless undertaking to try to sever this relation to the perceptive faculty from the notion of Beauty; therefore it is not sufficient for us to think of one as the effect of the other, but we must look upon both jointly and reciprocally as effect and as cause. In our pleasure in cognitions we distinguish without difficulty the passage from activity to passivity, and observe distinctly that the first ends when the second begins. In our pleasure in Beauty, on the other hand, no such succession between activity and passivity can be distinguished, and reflection is so completely intermingled with feeling that we believe ourselves to perceive form immediately. Beauty is therefore certainly an *object* for us, since reflection is the condition under which we have a sensation of it; but it is at the same time a *state of our personality*, since feeling is the condition under which we have a conception of it. It is then certainly form, because we contemplate it; but it is at the same time life, because we feel it. In a word, it is at once our state and our act.

And just because it is both these things together, it affords a triumphant proof that passivity by no means excludes activity, any more than matter does form, or limitation infinity—that consequently Man's moral freedom is by no means abolished by his necessary physical dependence. It proves this, and I must add, it is the *only* thing that can prove this to us. For as in the enjoyment of truth or of logical unity, perception is not necessarily one with thought, but follows the latter accidentally, so it can only prove to us that a rational nature can be followed by a sensuous one, and *vice versa*, not that both of them subsist together, not that they mutually influence each other, not that they are to be absolutely and necessarily combined. Rather, I would have to conclude the exact contrary from this exclusion of feeling, so long as there is thought, and of thought, so long as there is sensation—that is, the *incompatibility* of the two natures; and indeed the analytical thinkers are actually capable of adducing no better proof of the practicability of pure reason in human beings than that it is enjoined upon them. But as with the enjoyment of Beauty, or aesthetic unity, there occurs a real union and interchange of matter with form, and of passivity with activity, by this very occurrence the *compatibility* of both natures is proved, the practicability of the infinite in finiteness, and consequently the possibility of a sublime humanity.

We must therefore be no longer at a loss to find a passage from sensuous dependence to moral freedom, after we have seen, in the case of Beauty, that the two can perfectly well subsist together, and that in order to shew himself spirit Man does not need to eschew matter. But if he is already free in association with sensuousness, as the fact of Beauty teaches us, and if freedom is something absolute and suprasensible, as its very concept necessarily implies, there can no longer be any question how he came to rise from the limited to the absolute, to oppose sensuousness in his thought and will, since this has already occurred in Beauty. There can, in a word, no longer be any question how he passes from Beauty to Truth, since the latter by its very nature lies within the former; the question is rather how he makes his way from an ordinary actuality to an aesthetic one, from a sense of mere life to a sense of Beauty.

Twenty-sixth Letter

SINCE the aesthetic disposition of our nature, as I have explained in the foregoing letters, is what first gives rise to freedom, it may easily be realized that it cannot itself arise from freedom, and consequently can have no moral origin. It must be a gift of Nature; the favour of fortune alone can loosen the fetters of the physical condition and lead the savage to Beauty.

The germ of Beauty will as little develop where a niggardly Nature robs Man of every recreation, as where a prodigal one releases him from every exertion of his own—where dull sensuality feels no want, and where violent desire finds no satiety. Not where Man hides himself troglodyte-fashion in caves, eternally individual and never finding humanity *outside himself*; nor where he moves nomadically in great hordes, eternally plural and never finding humanity *inside himself*; only where he dwells quietly in his own hut, communing with himself and, as soon as he issues from it, with the whole race—only then will her lovely bud unfold. Where a limpid air opens the senses to every lightest contact and a vigorous warmth animates the exuberance of matter—where the sway of blind quantity is overthrown even in the inanimate creation, and triumphant form ennobles even the most degraded natures—in that joyful state and in that blessed zone where activity alone leads to enjoyment and enjoyment alone to activity, where sacred order springs forth from life itself and out of the law of order life alone develops, where imagination eternally escapes from reality and yet never goes astray from the simplicity of Nature—here alone will sense and spirit, receptive and creative power develop in the happy equilibrium which is the soul of Beauty and the condition of humanity.

And what sort of phenomenon is it that proclaims the approach of the savage to humanity? So far as we consult history, it is the same in all races who have escaped from the slavery of the animal state: a delight in *appearance*, a disposition towards *ornament* and *play*.

Extreme stupidity and extreme intelligence have a certain affinity with each other, that both seek only the 'real' and are wholly insensible to mere appearance. Only through the immediate presence of an object in the senses is the former shaken from its repose, and only through the referring of its concepts to the data of experience is the latter given repose; in a word, stupidity cannot rise above actuality and intelligence cannot remain stationary below truth. Insofar therefore as the requirements of reality and adherence to the actual are only the results of deficiency, indifference towards reality and interest in appearance are a real enlargement of humanity and a decisive step towards culture. In the first place they are evidence of an external freedom, for as long as necessity dictates and want impels, imagination is bound with strong chains to the actual; only when want is satisfied does it develop its unrestrained capacities. But they are also evidence of an internal freedom, since they reveal to us a force which sets itself in motion of its own accord, independently of any outward material, and possesses sufficient energy to repel the pressure of matter. The reality of things is the work of the things the appearance of things is the work of Man, and a nature which delights in appearance no longer takes pleasure in what it receives, but in what it does.

It is understood that I am here speaking only of aesthetic appearance, which is usually distinguished from actuality and truth, not of logical appearance, which is confused with them—of something which we love because it is show and not because we take it to be something better. Only the first is play, as the other is mere deception. To attach value to appearance of the first kind can never injure truth, because we are never in danger of substituting appearance for truth, which is after all the only way in which the latter can be injured; to despise appearance is to despise all fine art whatsoever, since appearance is its essence. Nevertheless it sometimes happens that the intellect presses its zeal for reality to such a pitch of intolerance as this, and utters a disparaging judgement about the entire art of beautiful appearance because it is mere appearance; but this only happens when the intellect recalls the affinity that I mentioned above. I shall have occasion some other time to speak in particular of the necessary limits of beautiful appearance.[1]

It is Nature herself that raises Man from reality to appearance, by endowing him with two senses which lead him through appearance alone to a knowledge of the actual. In eye and ear the importunacy of matter is already rolled away from the senses, and the object with which we have direct contact in our animal senses is withdrawn from us. What we *see* through the eye is different from what we *perceive*; for the intellect leaps out over the light to the objects. The object of touch is a force which we endure; the object of the eye and the ear is a form which we create. So long as Man is still a savage he enjoys merely with the senses of feeling, to which the senses of appearance are at this stage only subservient. Either he does not rise to seeing, or he is at any rate not satisfied with it. As soon as he begins to enjoy with the eye, and seeing acquires an absolute value for him, he is already aesthetically free also, and the play impulse has developed.

In the same fashion as the play impulse becomes active

[1] In the essay *On the necessary limits in the use of beautiful forms.—Trans.*

in him, and finds pleasure in appearance, there follows also the imitative creative impulse which treats appearance as something absolute. As soon as Man has once reached the point of distinguishing appearance from actuality, form from body, he is also in a position to dissociate the one from the other, for he has already done this by distinguishing between them. The capacity for imitative art is therefore generally given with the capacity for form; the urge to such art rests upon another aptitude which I need not treat of at the moment. How early or how late the aesthetic artistic impulse should develop will depend simply on the degree of fondness with which Man is capable of lingering at mere appearance.

Since all actual existence derives its origin from Nature, as an extraneous power, but all appearance comes originally from Man, as percipient subject, he is only availing himself of his absolute proprietary right when he separates the appearance from the essence and arranges it according to his own laws. With unrestrained freedom he can join together what Nature sundered, as soon as he can think of it together, and sunder what Nature combined, as soon as he can separate it in his intellect. Nothing need be sacred to him here but his own laws, if only he pays heed to the boundary which divides *his* territory from the existence of things, or Nature.

He exercises this human right of sovereignty in the *art of appearance*, and the more strictly he here distinguishes between the *mine* and the *thine*, the more carefully he separates shape from being, and the more self-dependence he is capable of giving to this shape, the more he will not merely extend the realm of Beauty but even secure the boundaries of Truth; for he cannot purify appearance from actuality without at the same time liberating actuality from appearance.

But he possesses this sovereign right positively only in the *world of appearance,* in the unsubstantial kingdom of the imagination, and only so long as he conscientiously abstains, in theory, from affirming existence of it, and renounces all attempts, in practice, to bestow existence by means of it. From this you see that the poet similarly steps outside his boundaries when he attributes existence to his ideal, and when he aims at some definite existence through it. He can only accomplish both these things either by infringing his poetic right, encroaching through his ideal upon the territory of experience and presuming to determine actual existence by the mere possibility of doing so, or else by surrendering his poetic right, letting experience encroach upon the territory of the ideal and confining possibility to the conditions of actuality.

Only insofar as it is *candid* (expressly renouncing all claim to reality), and only insofar as it is *self-dependent* (dispensing with all assistance from reality), is appearance aesthetic. As soon as it is deceitful and simulates reality, as soon as it is impure and requires reality for its operation, it is nothing but a base tool for material ends and can prove nothing for the freedom of the spirit. Besides, it is not at all necessary for the object in which we find beautiful appearance to be without reality, so long as our judgement about it pays no regard to this reality; for insofar as it does this, it is not aesthetic. Living feminine beauty will certainly please us just as well as, even somewhat better than, what is equally beautiful but only painted; but insofar as it pleases us better than the latter, it pleases us no longer as absolute appearance, it pleases no longer the pure aesthetic feeling; even the living pleases this feeling only as appearance, even the actual only as idea; but certainly it requires a further, and much higher, degree of liberal culture to perceive in the living itself only pure appearance, than to dispense with life in the appearance.

In whatever individual man or whole people we find this candid and self-dependent appearance, we may infer the presence of intellect and taste and every kindred excellence—there we shall see the ideal governing everyday life, honour triumphing over property, thought over physical satisfaction, dreams of immortality over existence. There will the voice of the people alone be held in awe, and an olive wreath bestow greater honour than a purple robe. Only impotence and perversity have recourse to false and necessitous appearance, and individual men as well as entire peoples who either 'help forward reality by means of appearance or (aesthetic) appearance by means of reality' —the tendency is to do both things together—reveal at the same time their moral worthlessness and their aesthetic incapacity.

To the question *how far appearance may exist in the moral world*, the answer is short and concise: *insofar as it is aesthetic appearance*, that is, appearance which neither seeks to take the place of reality nor needs to have its place taken by reality. Aesthetic appearance can never become a danger to moral truth, and where we find it happening otherwise, it can be shewn without difficulty that the appearance was not aesthetic. Only a stranger to fashionable society, for example, will interpret assurances of politeness, which is a universal form, as tokens of personal attachment, and when he is disappointed will complain of hypocrisy. But also only a duffer in fashionable society will, for the sake of politeness, call falsehood to his aid and flatter in order to be agreeable. The first still lacks the sense for absolute appearance, and therefore can give it significance only by means of truth; the second lacks reality, and he tries to make up for it by appearance.

Nothing is more common than to hear from certain petty critics of our age the complaint that all solidity has vanished from the world and that being is neglected for appearance. Although I feel by no means called upon to justify the age against this reproach, yet it is sufficiently clear from the wide range which these rigorous moralizers give to their indictment that they are finding fault with the age not merely for the false, but also for genuine appearance; and even the exceptions which they may chance to make in favour of Beauty concern rather the indigent than the self-dependent kind of appearance. They do not merely attack the specious gloss which hides the truth, which claims to be a substitute for actuality; they also fly into a passion with the beneficent appearance which fills out emptiness and covers up shabbiness, and with the idealistic appearance which ennobles a vulgar actuality. The duplicity of morals rightly shocks their rigid sense of truth; it is only a pity that they rank politeness as part of this duplicity. They dislike the way in which external glitter so often obscures true merit; but they are no less mortified that people should also demand appearance from merit, and do not exempt the internal contents from having an agreeable form. They miss the warm-hearted, robust and sterling qualities of former times; but they would also like to see established once again the uncouthness and bluntness of early manners, the clumsiness of ancient forms and the old Gothic extravagance. By judgements of this kind they shew a respect for material in itself that is not worthy of humanity, which ought rather to prize what is material only insofar as it is able to receive shape and to extend the realm of ideas. The taste of the century need not therefore pay much attention to such opinions, if only it can maintain its ground in other respects before a higher tribunal. Not that we are attaching value to aesthetic appearance (we have for a long time not been doing that sufficiently), but that we have not yet got as far as pure appearance, that we have not yet sufficiently separated existence from phenomenon, thereby securing the boundaries of both for ever—this it is with which a puritanical judge of Beauty might reproach us. And we shall deserve the reproach so long as we cannot enjoy the beauty of living Nature without coveting it, and cannot admire the beauty of representational art without asking its purpose—so long as we still concede to imagination no absolute legislation of its own, and fail to attribute to it its proper dignity through the respect which we shew to its works.

Twenty-seventh Letter

YOU need fear nothing for reality and truth if the lofty concept which I put before you in the last letter about aesthetic appearance should become universal. It will not become universal so long as mankind is still uncultivated enough to be able to abuse it; and if it were universal, this could only be effected by means of a culture which would at the same time make every such abuse impossible. To strive after absolute appearance demands greater capacity for abstraction, more freedom of heart, more vigour of will than Man needs if he confines himself to reality, and he must already have put the latter behind him if he wishes to arrive at appearance. How ill advised he would be, therefore, if he sought to follow the path to the ideal in order to spare himself the path to actuality! From appearance as we are here conceiving it, then, we should not have much to apprehend on behalf of actuality; all the more reason, therefore, to be apprehensive about actuality on behalf of appearance. Chained as he is to the material, Man has long since allowed appearance merely to serve his ends, before he has conceded it a personality of its own in the art of the ideal. For this purpose a total revolution is needed in the whole mode of perception, without which he would not find himself even on the right road towards the ideal. When therefore we discover traces of a disinterested free appreciation of pure appearance, we can infer some such revolution of his nature and the real beginnings in him of humanity. But traces of this sort are actually to be found already in the earliest crude attempts which he makes to *embellish* his existence—makes even at the risk of impairing it thereby in regard to its sensuous contents. As soon as he begins at all to prefer shape to material and to hazard reality for appearance (which, however, he must recognize as such), his animal sphere is opened and he finds himself upon a track that has no end.

Not content with what simply satisfies Nature and meets his need, he demands superfluity; to begin with, certainly, merely a superfluity *of* material, in order to conceal from his desires their boundaries, in order to assure his enjoyment beyond the existing need, but soon a superfluity *in* the material, an aesthetic supplement, in order to be able to satisfy his formal impulse also, in order to extend his enjoyment beyond every need. When he is simply collecting provisions for future use, and relishing them in advance in imagination, he is certainly trespassing beyond the present moment, but without altogether trespassing beyond time; he is enjoying *more*, not enjoying *differently*. But when at the same time he brings shape into his enjoyment, and becomes aware of the forms of the objects which satisfy his desires, he has not merely enhanced his enjoyment in scope and in degree, but also exalted it in kind.

Certainly Nature has given even to the creatures without reason more than the bare necessities of life, and cast a gleam of freedom over the darkness of animal existence. When the lion is not gnawed by hunger and no beast of prey is challenging him to battle, his idle energy creates for itself an object; he fills the echoing desert with his high-spirited roaring, and his exuberant power enjoys itself in purposeless display. The insect swarms with joyous life in the sunbeam; and it is assuredly not the cry of desire which we hear in the melodious warbling of the song-bird. Undeniably there is freedom in these movements, but not freedom from need in general, simply from a definite external need. The animal *works* when deprivation is the mainspring of its activity, and it *plays* when the fullness of its strength is this mainspring, when superabundant life is its own stimulus to activity. Even in mindless Nature there is revealed a similar luxury of powers and a laxity of determination which in that natural context might well be called play. The tree puts forth innumerable buds which perish without developing, and stretches out for nourishment many more roots, branches and leaves than are used for the maintenance of itself and its species. What the tree returns from its lavish profusion unused and unenjoyed to the kingdom of the elements, the living creature may squander in joyous movements. So Nature gives us even in her material realm a prelude to the infinite, and even here partly removes the chains which she casts away entirely in the realm of form. From the sanction of need, or *physical seriousness*, she makes her way through the sanction of superfluity, or *physical play*, to aesthetic play; and before she soars in the lofty freedom of the Beautiful above the fetters of every purposed end, she is already approaching this independence, at least from a distance, in the *free movement* which is itself end and means.

Man's imagination has, like his bodily organs, its free movement and its material play, in which, without any reference to shape, it simply delights in its absolute and unfettered power. Insofar as nothing of form is yet interfering with this play of fancy, and an unconstrained sequence of images constitutes its whole attraction, it belongs—though it is peculiar to Man alone—purely to his animal life, and only points to his liberation from every external sensuous constraint, without connoting as yet any independent creative power in him.[1]

From this play of the *free sequence of images*, which is still of a quite material kind and declares itself by simple natural laws, the imagination finally makes, in its attempt at a *free form*, the leap to aesthetic play. A leap we must call it, since a wholly new force now comes into play; for here, for the first time, the legislative faculty interferes with the operations of a blind instinct, subjects the arbitrary process of the imagination to its immutable and eternal unity, imposes its own self-dependence upon the variable and its infiniteness upon the sensuous. But so long

---

[1] The majority of games which are in vogue in ordinary life either depend entirely on this feeling of the free sequence of ideas, or at any rate derive their chief attraction from it. But little as it may point, in itself, to a higher nature, and readily as the most indolent souls are accustomed to yield themselves up to this free flow of images, yet this very independence of the fancy from external impressions is at least the negative condition of its creative capacity. Only as it turns away from actuality does plastic power rise to the ideal, and before the imagination can act according to its own law in its productive quality, it must already have liberated itself from extraneous law in its reproductive process. Certainly there is still a big step to be taken from mere lawlessness to a self-dependent internal system of law, and an entirely new power—the capacity for ideas—must at this point be brought into play; but this power can now develop with greater facility, since the senses are not working counter to it, and the indeterminate is bordering, at least negatively, on the infinite.

as crude Nature, which knows no other law than hurrying restlessly from variation to variation, is still too powerful, it will oppose that necessity by its fitful lawlessness, that stability by its unrest, that self-dependence by its indigence, that sublime simplicity by its insatiability. The aesthetic play impulse will then be hardly recognizable yet in its first attempts, as the sensuous impulse is incessantly interfering with its headstrong caprice and its savage appetite. Hence we see crude taste first seizing on what is new and startling, gaudy, fantastic and bizarre, what is violent and wild, and avoiding nothing so much as simplicity and quiet. It fashions grotesque shapes, loves swift transitions, exuberant forms, striking contrasts, glaring shades, pathetic songs. In this age beautiful means simply what excites a man, what gives him material—but excites him to spontaneous resistance, gives him material for possible fashioning; for otherwise it would not be the Beautiful, even for him. Thus a remarkable alteration has taken place in the form of his judgements; he seeks these objects not because they give him something to bear, but because they give him something to deal with; things please him not because they meet a need, but because they satisfy a law which speaks, albeit softly, in his breast.

Soon he is not content that things should please him, he wants to give pleasure himself, at first indeed only through what *belongs* to him, but finally through what *he* is. What he possesses, what he produces, may no longer wear upon it simply the marks of servitude, the uneasy form of its purpose; besides the service which it renders, it must at the same time reflect the genial intellect which conceived it, the loving hand which executed it, the serene and free spirit which chose and established it. Now the ancient German goes in search of glossier animals' skins, statelier antlers, more elegant drinking horns, and the Caledonian selects the choicest shells for his festivals. Even weapons may now be objects not simply of terror but also of delight, and the ornamented baldrick tries to attract as much attention as the deadly blade of the sword. Not content with bringing an aesthetic surplus into the necessary, the freer play impulse finally breaks completely away from the fetters of exigency, and Beauty for her own sake becomes the object of its endeavour. Man *adorns* himself. Free delight takes a place among his wants, and the superfluous is soon the chief part of his pleasures.

And just as form gradually approaches him from without, in his dwelling, his furniture, his clothing, it begins finally to take possession of Man himself, to transform at first only the outward but ultimately the inward man. The lawless leap of joy becomes a dance, the shapeless gesture a graceful and harmonious miming speech; the confused noises of perception unfold themselves, begin to obey a rhythm and weld themselves into song. While the Trojan host with shrill cries storms like a flight of cranes across the battlefield, the Greek army approaches quietly, with noble tread.[1] There we see only the arrogance of blind strength, here the triumph of form and the simple majesty of law.

A lovelier necessity now links the sexes together, and the sympathy of hearts helps to maintain the bond which was knitted only capriciously and inconstantly by desire. Released from its sullen chains, the quieter eye apprehends form, soul gazes into soul, and out of a selfish exchange of lust there grows a generous interplay of affection. Desire extends and exalts itself into love as mankind arises in its object, and the base advantage over sense is disdained for the sake of a nobler victory over the will. The need to please subjects the man of force to the gentle tribunal of

[1] Iliad, III, 1–9.—*Trans.*

taste; lust can be robbery, but love must be a gift. For this loftier prize he can contend through form alone, not through matter. He must cease to approach feeling as force, and to confront the intellect as a phenomenon; in order to please liberty, he must concede it. And just as Beauty resolves the conflict of natures in its simplest and purest example, in the eternal opposition of the sexes, so does she resolve it—or at least aims at resolving it—in the intricate totality of society, and reconciles everything gentle and violent in the moral world after the pattern of the free union which she there contrives between masculine strength and feminine gentleness. Weakness now becomes sacred, and unbridled strength disgraceful; the injustice of Nature is rectified by the generosity of the chivalric code. The man whom no force may confound is disarmed by the tender blush of modesty, and tears stifle a revenge which no blood could slake. Even hatred pays heed to the gentle voice of honour, the victor's sword spares the disarmed foe, and a hospitable hearth smokes for the fugitive on the dreaded shore where of old only murder awaited him.

In the midst of the awful realm of powers, and of the sacred realm of laws, the aesthetic creative impulse is building unawares a third joyous realm of play and of appearance, in which it releases mankind from all the shackles of circumstance and frees him from everything that may be called constraint, whether physical or moral.

If in the *dynamic* state of rights man encounters man as force and restricts his activity, if in the *ethical* state of duties he opposes him with the majesty of law and fetters his will, in the sphere of cultivated society, in the *aesthetic* state, he need appear to him only as shape, confront him only as an object of free play. *To grant freedom by means of freedom* is the fundamental law of this kingdom.

The dynamic state can only make society possible, by

curbing Nature through Nature; the ethical State can only make it (morally) necessary, by subjecting the individual to the general will; the aesthetic State alone can make it actual, since it carries out the will of the whole through the nature of the individual. Though need may drive Man into society, and Reason implant social principles in him, Beauty alone can confer on him a *social character*. Taste alone brings harmony into society, because it establishes harmony in the individual. All other forms of perception divide a man, because they are exclusively based either on the sensuous or on the intellectual part of his being; only the perception of the Beautiful makes something whole of him, because both his natures must accord with it. All other forms of communication divide society, because they relate exclusively either to the private sensibility or to the private skilfulness of its individual members, that is, to what distinguishes between one man and another; only the communication of the Beautiful unites society, because it relates to what is common to them all. We enjoy the pleasures of the senses simply as individuals, and the race which lives within us has no share in them; hence we cannot extend our sensuous pleasures into being universal, because we cannot make our own individuality universal. We enjoy the pleasures of knowledge simply as race, and by carefully removing every trace of individuality from our judgement; hence we cannot make our intellectual pleasures universal, because we cannot exclude the traces of individuality from the judgement of others as we do from our own. It is only the Beautiful that we enjoy at the same time as individual and as race, that is, as *representatives* of the race. Sensuous good can make only *one* happy man, since it is based on appropriation, which always implies exclusion; it can also make this one man only partially happy, because the personality does not share in it. Absolute good can bring happiness only under conditions which are not to be universally assumed; for truth is only the reward of renunciation, and only a pure heart believes in the pure will. Beauty alone makes all the world happy, and every being forgets its limitations as long as it experiences her enchantment.

No pre-eminence, no rival dominion is tolerated as far as taste rules and the realm of the Beautiful extends. This realm stretches upward to the point where Reason governs with unconditional necessity and all matter ceases; it stretches downwards to the point where natural impulse holds sway with blind compulsion and form has not yet begun; indeed, even on these outermost boundaries, where its legislative power has been taken from it, taste still does not allow its executive power to be wrested away. Unsocial desire must renounce its selfishness, and the agreeable, which otherwise allures only the senses, must cast the toils of charm over spirits too. Necessity's stern voice, Duty, must alter its reproachful formula, which resistance alone can justify, and honour willing Nature with a nobler confidence. Taste leads knowledge out of the mysteries of science under the open sky of common sense, and transforms the perquisite of the schools into a common property of the whole of human society. In its territory even the mightiest genius must resign its grandeur and descend familiarly to the comprehension of a child. Strength must let itself be bound by the Graces, and the haughty lion yield to the bridle of a Cupid. In return, taste spreads out its soothing veil over physical need, which in its naked shape affronts the dignity of free spirits, and conceals from us the degrading relationship with matter by a delightful illusion of freedom. Given wings by it, even cringing mercenary art rises from the dust, and at the touch of its wand the chains of thraldom drop away from the lifeless and the living alike. Everything in the aesthetic State, even the subservient tool, is a free citizen having equal rights with the noblest; and the intellect, which forcibly moulds the passive multitude to its designs, must here ask for its assent. Here, then, in the realm of aesthetic appearance, is fulfilled the ideal of equality which the visionary would fain see realized in actuality also; and if it is true that fine breeding matures earliest and most completely near the throne, we are bound to recognize here too the bountiful dispensation which seems often to restrict mankind in the actual, only in order to incite him into the ideal world.

But does such a State of Beauty in Appearance really exist, and where is it to be found? As a need, it exists in every finely tuned soul; as an achievement we might perhaps find it, like the pure Church, or the pure Republic, only in a few select circles where it is not the spiritless imitation of foreign manners but people's own lovely nature that governs conduct, where mankind passes through the most complex situations with eager simplicity and tranquil innocence, and has no need either to encroach upon another's freedom in order to assert his own, or to display gracefulness at the cost of dignity.

Index

'Abbāsids: 59
Absolute: 13–14, 31, 44, 52–3, 60, 68, 115–16
activity: 14
Addison (Joseph): 5
Aesthetica (Baumgarten): 5
aesthetic condition: 12–13, 99–103, 108–9, 112–13, 119, 124, 140
Aesthetic Letters (Schiller): 1–4, 7–10, 12, 14–18
aesthetic Man: 12, 108
aesthetics: 4–5
Agamemnon: 51
Alberti (Leone Battista): 17
Alexander the Great: 9, 58
Allgemeine Pädagogik (Herbart): 17
Anacreon: 107
apolaustics: 5
Apollo: 79
Apollo Belvedere: 9
appearance: 125–32, 140
Aquinas (Thomas): 36n.
Arabs: 58
Aristotle: 5, 8–9, 36n.
Art: as instrument of education, 9, 18; as instrument of morality, 11, 13; as play, 8; as spiritual service, 26; as 'torture', 24; cannot be debased by politics, 51; contrasted with science, 26; contrasted with Nature, 55; daughter of Freedom, 26; destroys wholeness and re-creates it, 45; enervating effect of, 13; free from human conventions, 51; related to character of age, 51–2; modes of enjoying it, 104–7, and see style; produces 'equipoise', 13
Artists (Schiller): 11
Athens: 39, 58
Aufhebung: 89n.

barbarians: 34, 55
Baumgarten (Alexander Gottlieb): 5, 9
Beauty: absolute value, 15; arises from two opposing principles, 81; as an imperative, 8; as a mystery, 25; as freedom from passion, 106; as living shape, 80; both object and state, 122; bracing and relaxing effect, 8–9, 82–8; confers social character, 138; energizing B., see energizing; ennobles sexual love, 28; equated with play, 78–9; expression of freedom in phenomena, 111; fetters and frees, 55; freedom of spiritual nature, 110; handmaid of culture, 12, 78; includes Truth, 123; indifferent to knowledge and will, 101, 108; in ideal and in experience, 82; instrument of morality, 57; leads from matter to form, 93; leads from sensation to thought, 92; makes Man whole, 138;

melting B., see melting; must precede freedom, 4, 27; necessary condition of humanity, 60; neither mere life nor mere form, 77, 80; no tendentious effect, 107; not found with heroic virtues, 59; not lawlessness but harmony, 90; object of play impulse, 76, 80; often accompanies moral depravity, 57–8; our second creator, 107; synthesis of Nature and Reason, 16; tempers wild life, 113; transitional value only, 15; twofold function, 55; union of reality and form, 81; work of free contemplation, 121

Boileau (Nicholas): 5
bracing effect of Beauty: 8
Bride of Messina (Schiller): 11
Burke (Edmund): 5, 9, 77n.
business man: 42
Butler (Professor E. M.): 10n.

cancellation: 88, 94
caprice: 14, 30, 34, 46
Catullus: 107
chivalry: 137
Church: 40, 47, 140
Commodus: 52
condition: 8, 60–1, 68
consciousness: 12
contemplation: 44, 78, 120
Corneille (Pierre): 5
Critique of Judgement (Kant): 2, 7–8
culture: 34–6, 39, 43, 50, 56, 68–9, 110, 115

dialectical thinking in Schiller: 16
Dalcroze (Jacques): 18
determinability: 91, 98
determinacy: 98, 100, 109
determination: 91, 98, 100, 109

Divinity: 61
duality in Kant and Schiller: 14
duty: 14, 31, 78, 111, 139

Education of Free Men (Herbert Read): 17
Education through Art (Herbert Read): 17, 18
energizing Beauty: 82–7
Eternal, the: 14

feeling: 12, 66, 117
feminine beauty: 128
Fine Art: 25, 51, 106
Fichte (Johann Gottlieb): 3, 6, 8, 13, 31n., 68n.
Finite, the: 14, 60
Florence: 59
Force: 47
formal impulse: 13–14, 65-78, 82, 93–4, 97, 119, see rational impulse
Foundation of the whole theory of science (Fichte): 68n.
Freedom: an absolute, 123; arises from opposition of necessities, 96; as aesthetic play, 15; brought by aesthetic disposition, 124, 137; contrasted with caprice, 14, 30; external and internal, 124; forming of the formless, 121; grounded in itself, 61; has its own laws, 109; Kantian view of, 15; means moral freedom, 12, 15; moral freedom and physical dependence, 122; moral freedom and sensuousness, 123; mother of Art, 26; must be preceded by Beauty, 4, 27; not found with sensuousness, 109; not subject to influence, 97; operation of Nature, not Man, 97; political freedom, 25
French Revolution: 4, 34-5

Friedrich Christian, Prince: 2–4, 7
Froebel (Friedrich): 18
fundamental impulses: 8, 13, 67, 94, 96–7

games: 134
genius: 58
God: 8, 14, 118
Gods of Greece (Schiller): 11
Goethe: 2–3, 6–8, 10, 52–5, 89n., 114
Gottsched (Johann Christoph): 5
Graces, The (ed. by Schiller): 3, 16, 19–20
Greeks: 9–10, 13, 37–40, 43, 51, 56, 58, 79–80, 121, 136

Hamilton (Sir William): 5
happiness: 112, 115–16
harmony: 13, 70n., 85, 111, 138
Hegel (Georg Wilhelm Friedrich): 11–12, 89n.
Hellenism: 9–10, 13
Herbart (Johann Friedrich): 17
Herder (Johann Gottfried von): 3
Highest Idea: 14
History of Antique Art (Winckelmann): 9
Horace: 49n.
Humboldts (Alexander and Wilhelm von): 3, 6
Hume (David), 9
Hymn to Joy (Schiller): 11

Ideal Man: 31–2
Iliad: 48, 136n.
inclination: 14, 31, 66, 78
indeterminacy: 98, 100, 102n.
Infinite, the: 14, 74
intellect: 39–40, 43–4, 70n., 107, 117, 126, 129, 140
Iphigenia in Tauris (Goethe): 114
Italy: 59

Jacobi (Fritz): 3
Jean Paul (J. P. Richter): 7

Juno: 79, 81
Jupiter: 49
justice: 67, 94

Kallias Letters (Schiller): 3, 7
Kant (Immanuel): 2–3, 5, 7–8, 11–12, 15, 24, 68n.
Klopstock (Friedrich Gottlieb): 3, 107n.
Körner (Christian Gottfried): 8

languid man: 84–7, 107
Laocoon of Rhodes: 9
Law: 8, 48, 52
Laws (Plato): 17
Lectures on the vocation of the scholar (Fichte): 31n.
Lessing (Gotthold Ephraim): 5, 9
Lombards: 59
London: 79n.

Madrid: 79n.
Man truly Man: 80
material impulse: 13–14, 70, 72, 77–8, 93–4, see sensuous impulse
Medicis: 59
melting Beauty: 59, 82–7
Mendelssohn (Moses): 9
Mengs (Raphael): 77n.
Messiah (Klopstock): 107
mind: 14
Modern Painters (Ruskin): 101n.
Montesquieu (Charles de): 9
moral condition: 113
moral instinct: 24
morality: 11
moral law: 117
moral Man: 12, 29, 46, 110
music: 105

Nature: absolute value, 15; acts for Man, 27; all-uniting, 39; as extraneous power, 127; as force and object, 120; as necessity, 97, 120; as sensibility, 72; as simplicity and truth, 47, 124; as spontaneity, 24; as substance, 32, 121; can be moral tyrant, 36; contrasted with Art, 54; contrasted with intellect, 14, 39; contrasted with Reason, 12, 16, 34, 37, 45, 74–5, 101, 118–19; contrasted with science, 90; decides what, not why, 110; demands multiplicity, 12, 32, 70n.; eight different meanings in *Letters*, 14; equated with feeling, 12; equated with God, 14; guide to morality, 24, 46; infinite Nature, 89–90; leads from material to beautiful, 109; lost through philosophy, 49; mere or crude Nature, 15, 37, 71n., 114, 135; mindless Nature, 133; mistress of the savage, 34; presses for reality, 65; raises Man from reality to appearance, 126; simplicity of Nature, 125; splendid profusion of Nature, 114; suppressed and controlled, 82

Necessity: 26–8, 97, 120, 139
Nero: 52
Nicomachean Ethics (Aristotle): 9, 36n.
nobility of character; 111n.
'Novalis' (Freiherr Friedrich von Hardenburg): 5

Object: 13
Olympia: 79
Olympus: 80
On grace and dignity (Schiller): 3, 7
On naïve and sentimental poetry (Schiller): 3, 7
On the art of tragedy (Schiller): 3
On the cause of pleasure in tragic objects (Schiller): 3
On the necessary limits in the use of

beautiful forms (Schiller): 126n.
On the sublime (Schiller): 3
'*On the sublime*' (Burke): see *Philosophical Enquiry*
ornament: 125

painting: 105
Paris: 79n.
passivity: 14
Pericles: 9, 58
person: 8, 60–1, 68
Person: 61
Pestalozzi (Johann Heinrich): 17
Philosophical Enquiry into the Origin of our Ideas of the Sublime and Beautiful (Burke): 77n.
philosophy: 49
Philosophy of Fine Art (Hegel): 11
Phocion: 58
physical condition: 113, 118–19
physical Man: 29, 46, 109
Plato: 5, 8, 16–18
play: 8, 13, 15, 78–80, 125–6, 133
play impulse: 8, 74–7, 79–80, 112, 126, 135
poetry: 11, 38, 105
politics: 26–7, 32–3, 40, 50–1
priesthood: 49
Protagoras (Plato): 17
Pythagoras: 50n.

rational impulse: 68–9, 96–7, see formal impulse
rational Man: 108
rational powers: 93
Read (Herbert): 16–18
Reason: abolishes natural State, 129; connected with formal impulse, 13; contrasted with Nature, 12, 16, 34, 36, 45, 74–5, 101, 119; contrasted with sensuousness, 14; decides forms of activity, 110; demands Absolute, 115; demands unity, 12, 32; discovers law, 48; equated with

consciousness, 12; equated with moral necessity, 98; exemplified by Greeks, 38; final State of Man, 12; had to be dismembered, 44; universality of consciousness, 95

relaxation: 13, 85

relaxing effect of Beauty: 8, 82

religion: 118

Renaissance: 17

Republics: 40, 140

Republic (Plato): 17

Roman Elegies (Goethe): 3

Romans: 52, 58

Rome: 79

Rousseau (Jean Jacques): 9, 20–1

Ruskin (John): 101n.

Saturn: 48, 120

savages: 34, 55, 124, 126

Schiller: earlier writings on aesthetics, 3, 7, 9, 12; influences, 2–3, 7–10, 24; intellectual qualities, 3, 5–7, 8–11, 14–16; letters to friends, 6–7, 55n.; personal qualities, 6–7, 9, 11–12, 15, 17; place in aesthetic philosophy, 4–6; works mentioned by name, 3, 7, 11, 126n.

Schlegels (August Wilhelm and Friedrich): 3, 5

science: 39, 51, 70n., 90

sculpture: 105

sense faculty: 63

sensuous impulse: 64–78, 82, 96–7, 118, 135, see material impulse

sensuous Man: 12, 87, 108–10

sensuousness: 13–14, 70, 97–8, 116–17, 123

sensuous powers: 93

sexual love: 28, 136

Shelley: 5

Socrates: 58

sophistry: 38

space: 92

Sparta: 58

speculation: 38–9, 42

Spirit: 14

spiritual Man: 87

spontaneity: 104, 111–12

State: aesthetic State the ideal of equality, 140; dynamic, ethical and aesthetic, 137–8; earliest condition of humanity, 28, 31, 33; end in itself, 33; moral State the human ideal, 12; must be repaired in motion, 29; must be morally transformed, 30; natural State abolished by Reason, 29, 35; natural State is chaotic, 42; natural State must become moral State, 29; natural State 'withers away', 12; rational State the human ideal, 12, 45–6; relationship to citizens, 32–3, 35, 41; rules by formula, 49; State of need contrasted with State of freedom, 34

statesmanship: 33

style in Art: 105

Substance: 14

Summa Theologica (Thomas Aquinas): 36n.

superfluity: 132

synthesis: 89

Synthesis aesthetic theory: 15

Taste: 12, 16, 56, 58, 84, 129, 135, 138

taut natures: 86

temporal Man: 31–2

tense Man: 84–7, 107

tension: 85

Thoughts on taste in painting (Mengs): 77n.

Three Levels aesthetic theory: 12, 15

Time: 52–3, 61–2, 65–7, 92, 103, 106
Titans: 121
tragedy: 13, 106
Trojans: 136
Truth: 52, 58, 67, 108
Tyranny of Greece over Germany (E. M. Butler): 10n.

Utility: 26

Venice: 79n.
Venus: 41, 79

Vienna: 79n.
Vittorino da Feltre: 17

Wagner (Richard): 5
Wie Gertrud ihre Kinder lehrt (Pestalozzi): 17
Wilhelm Meister (Goethe): 10
will: 94–5
Winckelmann (Johann Joachim): 9
Wisdom: 49
wit: 38

Zeus: 48, 120